MELT
&
POUR
SOAPMAKING

MELT
&
POUR
SOAPMAKING

MARIE BROWNING

Sterling Publishing Co., Inc.
New York

Prolific Impressions Production Staff

Editor: Mickey Baskett
Copy: Phyllis Mueller
Graphics: Lampe-Farley Communications, Inc.
Styling: Laney Crisp McClure
Photography: Patrick Molnar
Administration: Jim Baskett

Library of Congress Cataloging-in-Publication Data Available

    Browning, Marie.
       Melt & pour soapmaking / Marie Browning.
         p. cm.
       Includes index.
       ISBN 0-8069-2998-7
        1. Soap. I. Title: Melt and pour soapmaking. II. Title

       TP991 .B785 2000
       668'.12—dc21   00-058312

Published by Sterling Publishing Company, Inc.
387 Park Avenue South, New York, N.Y. 10016
Produced by Prolific Impressions, Inc.
160 South Candler St., Decatur, GA 30030
© 2000 by Prolific Impressions, Inc.
Distributed in Canada by Sterling Publishing
c/o Canadian Manda Group, One Atlantic Avenue, Suite 105
Toronto, Ontario, Canada M6K 3E7
Distributed in Great Britain and Europe by Cassell PLC
Wellington House, 125 Strand, London WC2R 0BB, England
Distributed in Australia by Capricorn Link (Australia) Pty. Ltd.
P.O. Box 6651, Baulkham Hills, Business Centre, NSW 2153 Australia

About the Author

Marie Browning is a consummate craft designer, making a career of designing products, writing books and articles, plus teaching and demonstrating. You may have already been charmed by her creative designs and not even been aware; as she has designed stencils, stamps, transfers, and a variety of other products for national art & craft supply companies.

You may also have enjoyed Marie's popular book entitled, *Beautiful Handmade Natural Soaps* published by Sterling Publishing in 1998. In addition to soapmaking, Marie has authored several other books published by Sterling, *Handcrafted Journals, Albums, Scrapbooks, & More* (1999), *Gifts From Your Garden* (1999), and *Memory Gifts* (2000). Her articles and designs have appeared in *Handcraft Illustrated*, **Better Homes & Gardens**, *Canadian Stamper*, *Great American Crafts*, *All American Crafts*, and in numerous project books published by Plaid Enterprises, Inc.

Browning earned a Fine Arts Diploma from Camosun College and attended the University of Victoria. She is a Certified Professional Demonstrator, a professional affiliate of the Canadian Craft and Hobby Association, and a member of the Stencil Artisan's League and the Society of Craft Designers.

Marie Browning lives, gardens, and crafts on Vancouver Island in Canada. She and her husband Scott have three children: Katelyn, Lena, and Jonathan.

Acknowledgments

Marie Browning would like to thank the following companies for their generous contributions of product, information, and support:

Environmental Technology Inc. (ETI)
South Bay Depot Road, Fields Landing, CA, USA
www.eti-usa.com
Top quality clear glycerin soap base, white coconut oil soap base, and liquid soap base. High heat soap molds, solid and liquid cosmetic grade colorants, top quality fragrance oils in 36 scents.

Martin Creative
2474 Oakes Road, Black Creek, BC, Canada
www.martincreative.com
High quality designer soap molds for hand-milled soaps, melt and pour soaps, and bath bombs

Delta Technical Coatings, Inc.
2550 Pellissier Place, Whittier, CA, USA
www.deltacrafts.com
Colored glycerin and white glycerin soap bases, fragrance oils, molds.

Yaley Enterprises
7672 Avianca Drive, Redding, CA, USA
www.yaley.com
Glycerin and coconut soap bases, solid colorants, fragrance oils, novelty soap molds, candle molds.

The Folk Art Connection
1209 Verdier Ave., Brentwood Bay, BC, Canada
www.folkartconnection.com
Melt and pour soap bases, fragrances and liquid colorants, soap molds, ingredients for bath salts, bath bombs.

I would also like to thank my family for all their understanding and support: Scott, Katelyn, Lena, and Jonathan.

Table of Contents

> *"If the day and night are such that you greet them with joy and life emits a fragrance like flowers and sweet scented herbs— that is your success. All nature is your congratulations."*
>
> Henry David Thoreau

Easy-to-make Recipes for Luxurious Soaps, Bath Salts, Bath Oils, Powders, and Bath Herbs

As technology speeds us up, we can try to stay balanced by slowing down and connecting with nature's colors, textures, sounds, smells, and elements. Home can be a place to renew and restore, a welcome retreat from the stresses of the world where you can unwind and balance mind, body, and spirit. Beautiful, natural bath products that engage the senses are small luxuries that pamper us and help make us happier and possibly healthier.

Commercial soaps and bath products are filled with harsh additives, fillers, and chemicals that are inharmonious with sensitive skin and can cause allergic reactions. While molded, natural soaps are expensive to buy, they are surprisingly easy to melt and pour at home. They contain no harsh detergents, only safe natural additives, and a minimum of preservatives.

It's never been easier to produce a fragrant, alluring bar of soap that is good for the skin and produces mounds of luxurious bubbles. Melt and pour soap bases make creating fine, rich coconut oil based soaps and clear, fun glycerin soaps quick and easy. Because the soap base can be melted in a microwave oven and cures immediately, it's possible to create and package a high quality product in a single day. The ease in producing your own molded soaps opens up many avenues for creativity in scenting and coloring.

This book provides recipes and techniques for creating your own handmade soaps (both melt and pour and hand-milled), bath salts, bath oils, powders, bath herb blends, and fragrant potpourri and sachets. It also includes ideas for devising your own creative blends and signature fragrance products, suggestions for packaging your creations, and ideas for creating elegant gift collections.

So close the door, and draw a warm bath. Dim the lights, hop in, and enjoy one of life's least expensive and easiest luxuries: a fragrant, relaxing bath. ✣

MARIE BROWNING

> *"The way to health is to take an aromatic bath and scented massage every day."*
>
> HIPPOCRATES

A Brief History of Soap

Soap has a long and interesting history, starting as far back as 2800 B.C. with the Babylonians. The first literary reference to soap is found in the 2nd century A.D. by the Greek physician, Galen. The ruins of a soap manufactory have been uncovered at Pompeii, but soap may have appeared even earlier, when prehistoric people discovered a slippery substance that made bubbles was created when fat and ash (an alkali) would meet and saponify when cooking over open pits.

Soap was savored by the Greeks, Romans, and Egyptians, who enjoyed communal baths and to whom fragrance products were an important part of everyday life. Ancient Egyptians regarded perfumes as the "sweat of the gods" and blended almonds, roses, frankincense, and myrrh. So skillful were their blends that ointments discovered in Tutankhamen's tomb in 1922 were still fragrant.

The popularity of bath houses and soap declined with the fall of the Roman Empire and did not return to Europe for several centuries. Soap re-entered general use as soapmaking guilds were formed in the 7th century. Olive oil based soaps, named "Castile soaps" after a region in Spain where olive trees grow, were made in southern Europe.

The basic bar of soap was processed further as manufacturers developed a method called milling. The basic soap was transformed by grating, melting, and mixing in additional oils, fragrances, and additives to greatly improve the qualities of the soap. Additionally, milled soaps were molded and decorated. Commercially produced triple-milled soaps from France are still considered the finest quality soaps available for their silky hardness, lasting fragrance, and excellent emollient characteristics. Many fragrant recipes created in past centuries for French royalty are still popular today. In home production, hand-milled soaps are equally exceptional performers but, lacking the large pressure rollers and grating facilities of manufacturing plants, they are more rustic in appearance. ✣

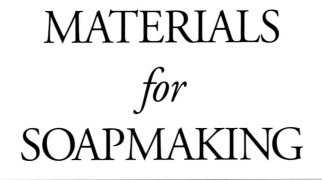

MATERIALS
for
SOAPMAKING

The ingredients and equipment needed to make melt and pour and hand-milled soaps are readily available at stores that sell crafts supplies, grocery stores, health food stores, and drug stores and can be ordered from catalogs. Many items may already be in your kitchen. This section introduces and discusses how to choose the materials you'll need to make soap and bath products at home, including:

Soap Bases
Fragrances
Additives
Colorants
Molds
Equipment

"The ordinary arts we practice every day at home are of more importance to the soul than their simplicity might suggest."

Thomas Moore

Soap Bases

Melt and Pour Soap Bases

There are three basic types of melt and pour soap bases: clear glycerin soap base, white glycerin soap base, and white coconut oil soap base. They all melt easily in a microwave oven or a double boiler and can be poured into decorative molds.

There are two main differences between melt and pour soaps and hand milled soaps. One, water is never added to melt and pour soap bases—it will make them slimy and prevent them from hardening properly. And two, melt and pour soaps set up immediately and need little curing time, enabling you to create handmade soaps almost instantly.

For best results and a high quality finished soap, purchase soap bases that are made with vegetable oils with no animal by-products, detergents, or fillers such as wax and alcohol.

Clear Glycerin Soap Base

Good quality glycerin soap base should be slightly cloudy, have a low sweet odor, and lather reasonably well. Good quality glycerin soap base should not contain wax, fillers, or alcohol and should leave your skin feeling clean and soft—not dry. High quality glycerin soap base should be gentle enough for all skin types and have a low scent ready for your own fragrant blends. If you wish a cloudy glycerin soap to be even more transparent when molded, simply melt, let harden, then re-melt before pouring into your

mold. Re-melting helps remove excess moisture from the soap. (It's the excess moisture that makes the soap look cloudy.)

White Glycerin Soap Base

Some "white coconut soap" bases available today are, in fact, glycerin soaps whitened with titanium dioxide and added coconut oil. The soap has a milky, translucent look and a lower melting point. When melted, the soap remains milky. It does not lather as much as a true white coconut soap.

Special care must be used when pouring clear glycerin soap base in a mold with white glycerin soap base. Having the same melting point makes the clear and white soaps blend together, with the white base migrating into the clear. For some soaps, such as chunk style soaps, this is an effect you don't want. To avoid this, use white coconut oil soap (which has a higher melting point) instead of white glycerin soap, or first place the white molded soap in the freezer to cool it before pouring the hot clear base over it. White glycerin soap does, however, make nice marbled effects when poured with a clear glycerin soap base.

White Coconut Oil Soap Base

A true coconut oil soap is made with coconut and vegetable oils. This pH balanced soap is enriched with vitamin E and makes your skin feel soft, clean, and healthy. The coconut oil creates a protective barrier that helps keep the skin supple. When melted, coconut oil soap base looks clear but turns bright white when fully hardened.

Using white coconut oil soap base enables you to create wonderful double-molded soaps and layered soaps. The brilliant white of this soap makes the colorants show up clear and true. You can melt clear glycerin soap base and white coconut oil soap together to make a nice translucent bar. Be aware, however, that it's a bit more difficult to remove the soap from the mold when soap bases are mixed. To remedy this, prepare the mold well with a mold release and when you're ready to unmold the soap, place the mold in the freezer for a few minutes to help release the soap.

Quality Considerations for Melt & Pour Soap Bases

Wax based fillers are added by some manufacturers to lower the cost of their glycerin and white based soaps. Generally, the cheaper the soap, the more wax and fillers it contains. Wax based fillers are much cheaper than other soap ingredients, and they greatly diminish the soap's cleansing qualities and lathering capabilities. Wax fillers also affect the smell, feel, and look of your finished soap. The more wax filler the soap contains, the harder the soap is to remove from the mold. Wax makes the soap very soft, and it does not last long in the bath—it quickly dissolves away.

Some companies also add alcohol to glycerin soap bases as a means of removing moisture, making the soap base more transparent. However, adding alcohol creates a strong smelling soap (the strong odor is hard to cover up with most fragrances) with safety and health problems. Alcohol is very flammable—microwave and stovetop fires have occurred when melting soap bases that contained alcohol. As the soap melts, the trapped alcohol becomes heated and expands and is easily ignited. Alcohol also is considered a skin irritant, and repeated use will dry out your skin. Soap made with alcohol should not be used by anyone who has sensitive skin or dry skin.

Base Soaps for Hand-Milled Soaps

Hand-milled soap recipes are included for those who are unable to locate the melt and pour bases or who prefer the harder, natural looking bars. Generally, using a higher quality base soap produces a higher quality hand-milled soap.

A soap base made with vegetable fats and lye and the cold process method of saponification works the best for hand-milled soaps. Cold process soapmaking is a complicated process—it's not easy and you need to have the right equipment. Unless you are prepared to take the time and effort to produce your own homemade soap base, use a natural soap purchased from a store or try and locate a small soapmaking enterprise (country and farmer's markets and craft fairs are good places to look) from whom you can order unscented vegetable soap bases. Pure olive oil soaps (Castile soaps) and natural vegetable oil based soaps that are available in fine gift stores and natural food stores also work well for hand-milling. Choose soaps without added fragrances, color, additives, and oils. Unscented and hypoallergenic soaps such as baby soaps also are good performers in hand-milled recipes.

Be aware that soap bars that are widely available in drugstores and supermarkets that are labeled "beauty bars," "deodorant bars," and "family cleansing bars" are not true soaps. The word "soap" does not even appear on the package! Today's commercial soaps are full of synthetic detergents, petrochemicals, and artificial preservatives that clog your pores and create dry skin. Their strong scents are hard to mask with essential or fragrance oils. These bars can be used for hand-milling, but the resulting soap will be of low quality. ❧

Fragrance

Adding fragrant oils is a significant part of creating your bath products. Although a lot of scent can come from the botanicals and additives, it will not be strong enough to create a beautiful aromatic product.

The two main types of oils are essential oils and fragrance oils. These are the raw fragrances used by perfumeries and cosmetic firms for blending scents and producing beauty and bath products. Good perfumes are so very expensive because long lasting, superior essential oils are used to make them. In the recipes in this book, I refer to both essential oils and fragrance oils as fragrance oils.

Let your budget and nose dictate what oils you purchase. **Never** use flavored extracts, potpourri oils, or candle scents in your soaps and bath products.

When you shop for fragrance oils, carry a small bag of freshly ground coffee to sniff. It will clear and refresh your sense of smell.

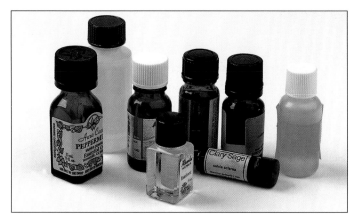

Essential Oils

The fresh scents of flowers and herbs are created by the essential oils produced by the plants. Of the many thousands of plants in the world, only about 200 produce essential oils used in the art of perfumery.

Capturing the fragrant essence of flowers has been performed since ancient times for fragrance, healing, and mood altering applications. The ancient Greeks and Romans produced fragrant ointments by immersing flowers, leaves, and woody stems in olive oil and animal oils, which drew out the scents. The Arabs were the first people to distill essential oils from plants. In distillation, plants are chopped and crushed, then heated with steam to force the volatile oils to vaporize. The essential oils then are condensed from the steam. The amount produced is very low, but the fragrance is very intense.

In Grasse, the perfume center of Provence in southern France, flowers are placed on layers of tallow until the fat absorbs the oils. This process is known as *enfleurage* and is used for delicate oils that cannot be distilled. It takes more than 2,000 rose petals to make a single gram of essential rose oil, while 2,000 lavender blooms produce 10 pounds of oil. This is why essential oils can vary in price from a few dollars an ounce to a few hundred dollars an ounce. Costly essential oils can be purchased diluted in a base oil that greatly reduces the price; the resulting oil is still strong enough to use in your fragrance products.

Essential oils are highly concentrated and must be diluted before they can be safely applied to the skin or blended into soaps. One percent (by volume) or less of an essential oil is considered a safe level for soapmaking. People with sensitive skin or allergies should be careful when using essential oils in their soap — too much essential oil can cause severe skin irritation.

Fragrance Oils

Fragrance oils are synthetically produced scenting oils and are much cheaper to produce than essential oils and are, therefore, less expensive. Since many fragrance oils are not derived from specific plants, they are available in a much wider range of scents and blends than essential oils and offer wonderful blends and floral scents that would be unattainable in an essential oil. Many high quality fragrance oils are actually blends of essential oils.

There is a wide range in the quality of fragrance oils available. When making soap, be sure to use fragrance oils that are not diluted with alcohol. Your nose can play a substantial role in determining the quality of the fragrance oil. Oils diluted with alcohol tend to smell alike and will have a sharp bite to them. Quality fragrance oils have a smooth, concentrated smell. When making soap, you need more of the lower quality diluted fragrance oil than you would a high quality fragrance oil to achieve the same result. Since less oil is required, good quality fragrance oils are a wise investment.

Fragrance oils with alcohol can also have a adverse effect on melt and pour soap bases. The alcohol pushes out moisture in the soap base in the form of white crystals.

Quality fragrance oils can be used for bath salts, bubble baths, sachets, and scented powders. Unlike pure essential oils which can be dangerous if used improperly, quality cosmetic-grade fragrance oils can be used safely with no fear of overuse.

Tips

- When adding fragrance to a hand-milled soap recipe, add the oils right before you pour the soap into the mold. If you add it too soon, the hot soap will evaporate most of it away.

- When making hand-milled soap, you'll need far less oil for scenting than you would if you were making soap from scratch. You can use drops of oil, rather than ounces, to successfully scent your soap.

- The amount of fragrance needed for each recipe will vary, depending on the scent you select (some oils are much stronger than others). Whatever the scent, make it stronger that you think you should, as some of it will dissipate.

- The fragrance and essential oils are the most expensive ingredients you will buy, but they are the most important. Do not buy cheap oils or extracts — you will be disappointed in the finished product if you do. ❧

Fragrance Blending

The magic of fragrance blending is a centuries-old skill that creates bottles of luxury and dreams. Blending your own scents to create endearing and lasting fragrant blends is not difficult if you follow a few basic steps. As you collect more oils, you can do more experimenting and creating. Many of the soap recipes in this book use combinations of fragrance oils to create distinctively enduring fragrant blends.

Scents in the perfume trade are categorized into scent groups. Knowing these groups greatly helps you to decide how your blends will evolve; for example, you may want a rose from the floral category with a slight spicy undertone of clove from the spice category. At right is a partial list of fragrances and the scent groups to which they belong. (Reasonably priced essential oils are marked with an asterisk [*].)

Elements of Fragrancing

Single scented perfumes that smell like natural botanicals, such as a freshly sliced orange or a fresh sprig of peppermint, are popular today. Although these scents smell like the original fruit, flower, or herb, they also contain other scents to make them lasting and

continued on page 16

Fragrance Groups

Citrus Scents	* Tea tree	Violet
* Bergamot	Rosemary	* Ylang ylang
* Grapefruit	* Sage	
* Lime		**Earthy Scents**
* Lemon	**Fruity Scents**	Amber
* Mandarin	Coconut	Frankincense
* Sweet orange	Green apple	Honey
* Tangerine	Kiwi	Musk
	Mango	* Patchouli
Spicy Scents	Melon	* Sandalwood
* Clove	Mulberry	
* Cinnamon	Pear	**Blended**
* Ginger		**Fragrances**
* Vanilla	**Floral Scents**	Baby Powder
	* Chamomile	Buttery maple
Herbal Scents	Jasmine	Cake bake
Bayberry	* Lavender	Chocolate
Cucumber	Lily of the valley	Honey almond
* Eucalyptus	Neroli	Ocean
* Peppermint	Rose	Rain
Pine		Sunflower

more charming. These different scents, called "notes," are broken down into three main elements:

Main scent — The key or predominant scent in the blend — the "high notes" or first aromas your nose detects.

Blenders — Additional scents to enhance the main scent. They are the "middle notes" of a blend.

Contrasting scents — These scents liven up the blend and provide the "low notes" that are the long lasting scents.

Considerations When Creating Blends

- The main scent is the overall aroma you wish to create, such as the tropical scent of coconut in the Soap on a Rope recipe on page 42. The blender scent that enhances and sweetens the main scent is ylang ylang. The contrasting scent is vanilla, which livens up the scent without overpowering the other scents but provides the lasting note.
- Some scents are natural blenders and mix well with scents from other categories. These blenders include lime, peppermint, lavender, rose, jasmine, sandalwood, vanilla, cinnamon, and honey.
- A fixative takes the place of the plant's cell structure and holds the scent. A fixative is necessary to help give the blend a long-lasting quality and release the fragrance moderately. The fixative can be unscented or add its own aroma to the blend. In fragrance crafting, the fixative can be the base soap, base oil, salts, or dried botanicals.
- You can easily test your fragrant blends by placing a few drops of oil on a paper towel. Let the fragrance oils blend for a few hours, then sniff to evaluate.
- Clear and refresh your sense of smell by sniffing a bag of freshly ground coffee when creating your blends.
- You will naturally choose scents that appeal to you. While some people enjoy the rich, exotic scents or warm, earthy scents, others will love the refreshing, clean scents of citrus or herbs.
- Experts recommend "layering" (washing, moisturizing, and spraying with complementary fragrances) to make scents last longer.
- Dry skin does not hold a fragrance as well as skin that is well hydrated.
- Your skin's pH and the oil content of your body will alter the scent slightly, creating your own individual odor.

Aromatherapy

Aromatherapy is rooted in herbal and folk medicine traditions. The ancient Egyptians, Greeks, Romans, Hebrews, Indians, and Chinese documented the use of fragrances for cosmetic and medicinal purposes. Aromatherapy came to North America from Europe, where physicians and cosmetologists explored the therapeutic benefits of essential oils for treating medical and psychiatric disorders.

While no medical claims can be made, it is believed that essential oils, referred to as the "soul" or "spirit" of plants, affect us emotionally, physically, and aesthetically. And it is certainly no surprise that a relaxing, scented bath can soothe us and renew our spirit.

It's not clear how much aromatherapy has to do with aroma and how much it has to do with the other properties of the oils. For this reason, I use both essential oils and synthetic fragrance oils in my beauty product recipes. The fragrance oils offer a wide selection of scents that would be unattainable if only essential oils were used.

Effects & Qualities

- Peaceful and relaxing scents - lavender, sandalwood, honeysuckle and chamomile, ylang ylang, tangerine, rose, lemon verbena
- Energizing - rosemary, peppermint, lemon, lime, jasmine, honey
- Stimulating and uplifting - bergamot, orange, jasmine, rosemary, lemon verbena, mints, sage, pine

- Antiseptic properties - tea tree, eucalyptus, peppermint, lavender
- Focusing, head-clearing scents - frankincense, peppermint, grapefruit, cinnamon, chamomile, lavender, orange, ylang ylang

Virtues of a Bath

A fragrant bath is a perfect way to improve your mood. A bath engages almost all the senses, allowing you to respond to visual, olfactory, tactile, thermal, and auditory cues. Try adding other sensory experiences to the bath ritual (fragrant bubbles, ocean sounds, flickering candlelight) to aid relaxation.

- To relax, draw a warm bath (a hot bath can be drying to the skin). Light some candles and incense. Use some calming scents. This will help you slip into a tranquil, restful sleep.
- A stimulating, cool bath increases circulation and refreshes. Use fresh herbal scents to soothe tired muscles.
- Uplift your psyche with energizing citrus and honey scents. Add sounds of the ocean and fun bubbles.
- For a romantic evening, draw a warm bath, add classical music and pampering, warm fragrances. Place a vase of fresh roses in the room. Add rose petals to the tub.
- For a morning wake-up, shower with an uplifting or stimulating soap.

Natural Additives

Oatmeal, dried herbs, and extra oils can be added to soaps to nourish and soft005en and for their gentle scrubbing properties. The additives I recommend are generally considered to be safe and will help you make your soap interesting when you use the recommended amounts. Find these additives at grocery stores, health food stores, and craft supply outlets.

Almonds — Finely ground almonds, a natural exfoliant, can be added to melt and pour soap bases and hand-milled soap for their slight bleaching action and gentle abrasive qualities that help cleanse skin and improve circulation. Ground almonds also add a pleasant nutty fragrance. They can be used toasted or raw.

Bee pollen — A fun, colorful additive, purported to be energizing and uplifting, that imparts a sweet honey-floral aroma. Bee pollen will dissolve in the bath. It's believed that grains of bee pollen in soap can help desensitize hay fever sufferers.

Beeswax — A highly fragrant natural animal wax from the honeycomb of the honey bee. Beeswax has a golden amber color and makes your bars softer to the touch with a slight pleasant sent of honey. It is valued in cosmetics for emulsifying creams and ointments. For hand-milled soap recipes, add the melted wax near the beginning of the melting process and stir well. Beeswax can be added to melt and pour soap bases in small quantities at the beginning of the melting process, but if the wax cools in the soap base before it's thoroughly blended, you will end up with hard bits in your soap. If you put too much beeswax in a melt and pour soap, the beeswax makes the soap very soft and difficult to remove from the mold. Beeswax also can make soap lather less.

Cardamom — Native to Asia, cardamom has a fresh, warm spicy scent. When added to soaps, finely ground cardamom improves circulation and is warming, uplifting, and energizing.

Pictured top row left to right: almonds, ground; bee pollen, beeswax; cardamom seeds; cinnamon, ground and whole. *Second row left to right:* citrus peel; cloves, whole; cocoa butter; cornmeal; green tea; luffa sponge. *Third row left to right:* mica; oatmeal; poppy seeds; rosemary. *Bottom row left to right:* sage; seaweed; vitamin E capsules; wheat bran.

Cinnamon — Both powdered cinnamon and whole cinnamon sticks are useful in fragrance crafting. Powdered cinnamon adds a warm, spicy scent and a soft speckled brown color to soaps. Using too much will make your soap scratchy. Cinnamon works as an astringent and a stimulant in bath products and is believed to reduce stress. Cinnamon sticks can be a creative decorative touch for packaging or in potpourri blends.

Citrus peel — Ground dried lemon, orange, or lime peel is cleansing, astringent, and a refreshing aromatic addition to soap.

Cloves add a hot, spicy scent that is uplifting and mentally stimulating. Use very small amounts — it can be irritating to sensitive skin.

Cocoa butter is a fat that comes from the crushed seeds of the cacao tree and is separated during the process of making cocoa. It is solid at room temperature but melts at body temperature. Cocoa butter, when added to soaps, improves the soap by making it creamy and hard. It is also a good emollient and conditioning oil. Cocoa butter is used in making fine chocolates, so look for it at candy supply stores.

Cornmeal can be added to hand-milled soaps and melt and pour soap bases — it's a gentle abrasive and stimulant. It imparts a nice straw coloring to soap and will not alter the scent of the soap.

Distilled water — If you live in an area that has hard water (hard to make soap suds), you may wish to use bottled distilled water in your hand-milled soaps. Water is never added to melt and pour soap bases.

Glycerin, a product of the saponification process, is a compound of carbon, hydrogen, and oxygen. It is a clear, colorless, oily, sticky liquid. Glycerin is widely used in the cosmetic industry as an emollient and can be added to hand-milled or melt and pour soaps. In bubble bath formulas, glycerin gives the bubbles elasticity and lasting power. In bath salts, glycerin adds a glistening touch and also helps the salts from drying out the skin.

Green tea — Both green and black teas come from the *Camellia sinensis* bush. Green teas are made from leaves that are picked and dried. Black teas are made with leaves that have been cured (oxidized) or toasted. All teas contain healthful substances; green tea is rich in antioxidants, flavonoids,

Lavender

Lemon verbena

Chamomile

and indoles — substances that boost immunity and are proven disease fighters. Green tea is linked to a number of health benefits — not only by drinking it but also by experiencing its exhilarating and rejuvenating fragrance.

Honey is produced by bees from the nectar gathered from flowers. Its main components are water and sugar, but there are also small amounts of organic products, such as essential oils of the flowers. It is these trace elements that are thought to give honey its curative properties. Honey is an excellent emollient and a nice addition to hand-milled soap and melt and pour soap bases. Too much honey will make the bars soft. A facial mask of pure honey helps to disinfect and soothe minor skin irritations and dryness, and honey can help heal burns and soothe sore throats — it contains a germ-killing substance called inhibine that helps prevent infection. Honey in your soap and bath products provides a healthy uplifting quality and helps you relax. Caution: Bath products containing unpasteurized honey can be hazardous to infants. Use only pasteurized honey in products intended for use on babies.

Lavender — One of the most widely used herbs in personal cleansing throughout history. Dried lavender buds add a relaxing, healing, and aromatic element to your soapmaking.

Luffa (or loofah) sponge (*Luffa cylindrica*) is a gourd that looks like a fat cucumber. (It is, in fact, related to the cucumber and is easy to grow.) The ripe fruit is soaked, beaten to remove the seeds, then dried. The fibrous skeleton that is left makes a wonderful bath sponge suitable for even the most tender skins. Scrubbing with a luffa improves circulation. Whole slices or small, chopped up bits can be added to soap bases.

Mica pigment powders — Non-toxic mica pigments can be added to soaps to create sparkles or a metallic luster. You'll need only a very small amount. It's a good idea to mix 1/2 teaspoon of a powdered pigment with 2 oz. of glycerin and dispense into your liquid, melted soap by the drop from a plastic squeeze bottle.

Oatmeal gently soothes sensitive or irritated skin and is beneficial to most skin types. Add whole or finely ground oatmeal to melt and pour or hand-milled soap bases. Use only regular (long-cooking) oats in fragrance crafting.

Olive oil — A very fine, strongly scented rich oil that is very good for sensitive skin. Use cold pressed, extra-virgin olive oil for fragrance crafting. It is useful as a healing and soothing bath oil when blended with other base oils. It brings stable lather and emollient and conditioning qualities to soaps. In Castile soap, olive oil is the main fat.

Poppy seeds add gentle abrasive qualities for stimulating and cleansing the skin. They also can add a decorative element (such as simulating seeds in strawberry soap). Use only a small amount.

Powdered milk — Milk is a natural cleanser and is an excellent addition to hand-milled soaps and melt and pour soap bases. I like to mix powdered milk with honey or oils before adding to the melted soap to better incorporate it. It will soften the soap slightly, so do not use too much. Use instant powdered milk; the non-instant kind doesn't dissolve readily.

Rosemary — Dried, whole rosemary is stimulating and soothing and helps to improve circulation when added to your soap. The refreshing herbal scent is also uplifting.

Shea butter, from the nut kernel of the shea tree, native to Africa, is used as a moisturizer and in suntan and massage creams. It is added to hand-milled and melt and pour soaps for superfatting; it will not saponify in cold process soapmaking.

Seaweed restores and helps to smooth skin. The dried Nori seaweed sold in supermarkets for making sushi works fine for soapmaking.

Vitamin E oil is an excellent healing oil for burns and scrapes when used in soaps and bath oils. It is also an exceptional antioxidant and natural preservative in fragrant bath oils where botanicals have been added for decoration. I use vitamin E oil in hand-milled soap recipes when fresh fruit or vegetables are used as additives. Vitamin E can be found in capsule or liquid form; capsules are less expensive. For the recipes in this book, I used vitamin E capsules as a preservative; simply cut or pierce the capsule and squeeze out the oil.

Wheat bran — A very gentle exfoliant, wheat bran adds bulk, texture, and interesting brown speckles to soaps.

Considerations When Choosing Additives

- Just because an ingredient is natural, it doesn't mean it is safe to use in your soap.
- Too much additive may soften your soap or make it scratchy and uncomfortable to use.
- When properly preserved and treated, fresh fruits and vegetables can be used in hand-milled soaps.
- Don't use fresh, organic materials from vegetables and fruits in melt and pour soap bases.
- If additives are not properly dried or preserved, they can cause your soap to become rancid.
- Beware of additives that make the soap look good without any added benefits or that just seem impractical. For example, commercial potpourri may look good sprinkled in a clear soap, but the large petals will clog your drain and scratch your skin, and commercial potpourri may contain ingredients that would be extremely dangerous to use on your body.

(see page 90 for other botanical additives)

"And the men themselves waded into the sea and washed off the dense sweat from skin and shoulder and thigh. Afterwards...when...the inward heart has been cooled to refreshment, they stepped into the bathtubs smooth-polished, and bathed there, and after they had bathed and anointed themselves with olive oil, they sat down to dine..."
FROM THE ILIAD

Colorants

Color is an important ingredient of a soap's allure. Use spices and dried herbs for a natural-colored soap or cosmetic grade colorants for a brightly colored bar.

Natural Powders

Soaps colored with natural powders have a country look with attractive warm brown and tan hues. Natural powders also add interesting colors and textures to your soap.

Cocoa powder — Add cocoa powder to a small amount of an oil additive before mixing — the result will be a light, warm brown. If you add too much, it will affect the overall aroma.

Dried herbs — Dried parsley flakes, lavender buds, and other herbs add little bits of color to your soaps. Be careful to use only safe, recommended herbs. (See the list on page 90.)

Ground spices — Ground cinnamon, cardamom, allspice, clove, and star anise can be added for color as well as for fragrance. They contribute warm brown

speckles to soaps. Turmeric adds a golden, orange hue and a very little paprika adds a peachy tone with red specks. Purchased powdered spices can be used, but for maximum strength and freshness, grind your own whole spices in a spice mill or coffee grinder and sift through a fine sieve before adding to the soap. Be careful not to add too much or your soap will be scratchy.

Mica powders and flakes — Mica powders give a beautiful sheen and are available in a wide selection of metallic colors. The U.S. Food and Drug Administration does not restrict the use of mica flakes and powders in soaps; however, a mask is recommended when working with the powder.

Cosmetic Grade Colorants

Available in both solid and liquid forms, colorants are found in the fragrance crafting departments of craft stores and are available from soapmaking suppliers.

Solid colorants — in a soap base are especially easy to use — they melt with the soap base. Color disks are recommended for beginners and when working with children. Six colors are available in solid disks — red, blue, yellow, orange, green, and black. It is easy to blend them to create more colors.

High quality, liquid cosmetic grade colorants create true, clean colors and are excellent for blending and creating many

different hues. Liquid cosmetic colorants can be used for coloring soap as well as bath salts, bubble bath, bath oil, and candles. Liquid colorants come in the same colors as solid colorants (red, blue, yellow, orange, green, and black). Unlike food coloring, which is water-based, liquid cosmetic colorants mix with the oils in soaps and oil-based products beautifully and they will not stain your skin like food coloring does, even when rubbed on full strength. *Please note:* The amounts of colorants in the recipes in this book are based on the number of drops of cosmetic grade liquid colorants.

Food Coloring

Food coloring is not suitable for soaps (the color quickly fades) or for bath oils (the dye is not soluble in oil and just sits on top of the oil as floating beads of concentrated color). You can, however, use small amounts of food coloring to tint bath salts and bubble bath.

Considerations When Adding Colorants

- When colorants are added to hand-milled soap, the hue will lighten as the soap cures.
- Because the results can vary depending on the size of the drop or the number of drops of colorant you use, take notes while mixing colors and record your results.
- Colorants appear clear and jewel toned in clear glycerin soap bases, but in white soap bases they are softer pastels.

Color Mixing Basics

To understand color mixing and theory, you need to know a few basic principles. The best way to learn, however, is through experience and experimentation. Purchase a color wheel which will help show the relationships between colors.

Primary colors, the base colors from which all other colors are derived, are red, blue, and yellow. **Secondary colors**, which are mixes of primary colors, are green (yellow + blue), purple (red + blue), and orange (red + yellow).

Intermediate colors (sometimes called "tertiary") are obtained by mixing of a primary color with a neighboring secondary color — for example, yellow green (lime green) is a mixture of yellow and green.

Complementary colors are colors that are opposite one another on the color wheel — red is the complement of green, purple is the complement of yellow, blue is the complement of orange. When you mix a color with its complement, you dull or mute the color, making it less intense. Some examples include dusty plum (purple + a touch of yellow) and golden ocher (yellow + a touch of purple).

Shades are darkened colors, created by adding black.

Tints are lightened colors, created by adding white. (Pink, a mix of red + white, is a tint of red.)

Moods of Colors

Colors, like scents, trigger positive and negative emotions and affect our moods. Here are some recognized positive sensations associated with colors:

Red, crimson — Stimulating, passionate, and arousing. Intense, powerful, hot.

Pink, rose — Soft and delicate. Feminine, sweet.

Orange, amber — Exciting, invigorating, jovial, exuberant, bright, stimulating, cheering, comforting, secure.

Coral — Mellow, glowing, balancing.

Brown — Earthy, natural, comforting, stable, refined, soothing.

Yellow — Sunny, electric, enlightened, bright, energizing, cheerful, life giving, joyous.

Gold, ochre — Warming, enriching, enhancing, creative.

Green, emerald — Relaxing and restful (think of nature, freshness, and health) — it's the new neutral that all other colors look good beside. Wealth, balance, tranquil, refreshing, sensitive.

Celadon — Restful.

Lime green — Refreshing, natural.

Blue, sapphire — Calming and relaxing, restful, trusting, comfortable, cool; lowers blood pressure.

Light blue — Misty, cooling.

Aquamarine — Stimulating, cheerful.

Violet — Subduing, imaginative, romantic, enchanting, rich, royal, charming.

Deep plum — Spiritual.

White — Light, celestial, innocent, pure, clean, good.

Cream, parchment, ecru — Warm, simple, harmonious.

Black — Luxurious, powerful, elegant, dignified, mysterious.

Gray — Neutral, quiet, calm. ✤

Molds

Molds help you make your hand-milled soaps, melt and pour soaps, and solid fizzing bath salts appear more professional and fancy. Soap molds are available in traditional and fun shapes.

Suggested Molds for Soap

High heat plastic soap molds are designed for soap and are overall the best and safest for soapmaking. Their deep, clean smooth contours allow you to safely create professional looking soaps that de-mold easily. They are designed for repeated use and stand up to the high temperatures of melt and pour soap bases without warping or melting. The molds are available in single shapes or in trays of fancy motifs. There are also very small shapes designed especially for making chunk style soaps. Look for good quality soap molds that don't require pre-treatment and for trays that are self-leveling. You'll find high heat molds at craft stores.

Individual resin casting molds are an excellent size and depth for single bars of soap. The number of ounces of melted soap the mold holds is stamped on the bottom of each mold.

Plastic food storage containers — Small sandwich or storage containers (4" x 6") will accommodate the hand-milled or loaf style soaps. Try to find ones with rounded corners and no design on the inside bottom. Choose a plastic container that's dishwasher safe — you don't want to use one that will melt and collapse from the high temperature of the melted soap, causing a spill. Always stir the soap a bit before pouring in a plastic food storage container to help it cool down.

PVC (polyvinyl chloride) pipe — Pieces of PVC plumbing pipe 1-1/2" to 3" in diameter make beautiful rounds of soap that fit nicely in the palm of your hand. Pipe molds are inexpensive and easy to use. Use a saw to cut a piece of pipe 6" to 7" long. Sand the cut edges smooth. Treat well with a mold release before each use. Seal the bottom of the pipe mold so the soap doesn't run out by placing three or four layers of plastic wrap on one end. Use strong rubber bands to snugly hold the plastic wrap in place. To unmold the soap, remove the plastic wrap and push the soap through, using a bottle with a slightly smaller diameter than the mold.

Plastic candle molds — There is a wide variety of plastic candle molds available: three dimensional molds, pyramid molds, square molds, and molds for wax ornaments. Because candle molds are designed to take the high temperatures of melted wax, they can stand up to hot melted soap. It's difficult to remove soap from some candle molds, however. Choose low, wide molds rather than long, skinny molds. **Always** use a mold release.

Metal candle molds — can handle the high temperatures, but most soap bases reacts with metal, especially aluminum. This reaction causes the metal to corrode quickly, which in turn discolors your soap. The corrosion eventually can destroy metal

Preparing PVC mold with mold release.

molds. If you use metal molds, be sure to use a mold release.

Plaster and candy molds — cannot take the high temperatures of melt and pour soap bases. If hot melted soap is poured into them they collapse, spilling their contents. Deep candy and plaster molds are, however, suitable molds for hand-milled soaps and solid fizzy bath salts.

Plastic ice cube trays — can melt and warp if the soap is too hot. They also need to be treated with a mold release.

Plastic containers — the type designed to keep food from crushing — are tempting because of the wonderful designs and deep shapes, but the plastic can warp and melt when hot soap is added. Most **plastic cups** also are unsuitable for soapmaking.

Rubber latex molds — You can make your own signature molds for soapmaking with liquid latex mold builder available at craft stores. Use the brush-on rubber mold builder to make molds from natural objects such as pebbles and shells or manufactured objects such as figurines and ornaments. Look for the white latex rubber that dries to a translucent amber color; red rubber may transfer the color to the soap.

Wooden molds — have been used since the invention of soap. Wood soap molds are affected by the moisture and will eventually need to be replaced.

Mold Releases

Using mold releases makes it easier to remove the hardened soap from a mold. **Always** use a mold release if the recipe recommends one.

Petroleum jelly is a fatty, translucent substance that is a by-product of the petroleum industry. It is widely used in cosmetics as an emollient and barrier cream. It's an excellent mold conditioner that won't leave a sticky residue on the soap. Rub a thin film of petroleum jelly on the inside of hard molds (PVC pipe, wood, and metal ones) to ensure easy soap removal.

Vegetable oil — in liquid and spray forms also works as a mold release. But even a thin film of oil on the mold can make the soap feel a bit greasy, and the oil can become rancid over time, altering the fragrance of the soap.

TIP: If you're having trouble getting the soap out of a mold, place it in the freezer until thoroughly chilled, then release.

Equipment

Many tools and pieces of equipment for creating melt and pour and hand-milled soaps are items that you may already own and have in your kitchen. If you clean glass and metal tools thoroughly after soapmaking, they can be returned to the kitchen for use in food preparation.

Glass measuring cups — 1 cup, 2 cup, and 4 cup heat resistant glass (such as Pyrex) measuring cups are used to measure grated soap, additives, salts, and other ingredients. They are the best containers for melting soap bases in the microwave and the pouring spouts make it easy to pour soap into the molds.

Heat resistant glass bowl — You will need an 8 cup heat resistant glass (such as Pyrex) measuring bowl and a large saucepan (any metal is fine) to make a double boiler for melting grated soap for hand-milled soaps or for melting soap bases on the stove. Simply put water in the saucepan and place the bowl in the water.

Glass mixing bowls — Large glass bowls are useful for blending bath salts, holding grated soaps, and blending dried botanicals.

Measuring spoons — You'll need a set of good metal measuring spoons for measuring smaller amounts of ingredients.

Glass droppers — You will need three or more glass eye droppers for measuring fragrance oils. Do not use plastic droppers — some essential oils will eat right through them, and because you can't wash out the scent from a plastic dropper, you can contaminate your oils by mixing the scents.

Grater — A simple, inexpensive kitchen grater is needed to grate soap for hand-milling.

Food processor — A food processor can further process grated soaps for a smoother soap and quicker melting. Softer soaps especially benefit from further processing. Make sure your processor bowl is clean and dry. Never add water when processing your soap.

Electric spice and coffee grinder — Useful for grinding small amounts of additives such as almonds or oatmeal and for grinding whole spices. Clean after each use by grinding a piece of fresh bread or some rice — the bread or rice soaks up any remaining oils. Wipe out the grinder with a paper towel.

Mixing spoons — Metal kitchen spoons are needed to mix melted soap, bubble bath, bath salts, and other blends. Metal spoons will not transfer fragrances, so they are safe to use for food after cleaning. If you use wooden spoons, clearly mark them "FOR FRAGRANCE CRAFTING ONLY" — the wood will retain scents and transfer them to food.

Drying rack — Useful for drying and curing hand-milled soaps — it allows air to circulate and prevents the soap from warping. If you can't find a wooden rack, a metal rack will do.

Wax paper — You need wax paper for making solid fizzing bath salts. Wax paper is also useful to protect your work area when pouring melt and pour soaps.

Water mister — A mister with a fine spray is needed for the liquids when making solid fizzing bath salts.

Sharp knives — For cutting melt and pour soap bases in smaller pieces and for slicing finished molded soaps. A variety of sizes, from small paring knives to large butcher knives, are handy.

Small plastic funnel — For bottling liquid bath products. It keeps the liquid away from neck of the bottle, making a more secure fit for your cork.

"The earth laughs in flowers."

Ralph Waldo Emerson

Terms

Abrasives — Substances that, when used in soap, gently scrub the skin for a gentle cleansing action. Examples: cut luffa sponge, ground almonds.

Additives — Ingredients added to soaps that impart special characteristics to the finished bar. Example: the addition of extra oils to create a superfatted soap that's extra moisturizing, richer, and milder.

Antiseptic — A substance that inhibits growth of bacteria on living tissue and in the product. Example: botanicals such as lavender.

Aromatherapy — The therapeutic use of aromas (usually from essential oils) to affect emotional and physical well being.

Aromatic — Having a fragrant taste and/or smell.

Astringent — In cosmetic terms, a substance that contracts the pores and tissues, making the surface smoother.

Blenders — In fragrance crafting, the scents that are combined with the main scent to enhance and fix into a single blended fragrance. Blenders give harmony and maintain the overall balance of a blended fragrance. Example: in a spicy rose scent, rose is the main scent, cinnamon and clove are blenders.

Detergent — A cleanser made with petroleum distillates rather than natural fats.

Emollient — An ingredient that moisturizes the skin, smoothes wrinkles, improves skin elasticity, and protects the skin. Examples: glycerin, almond oil.

Enfleurage — An age-old method of extracting essential oils using odorless fats and oils to absorb essential oil from a plant.

Essential oils — Volatile and fragrant oils produced in various parts of flowers and herbs. High quality essential oils impart the beneficial qualities of a plant to your fragrance product. Example: lavender essential oil is stimulating and invigorating.

Exfoliants — See "Abrasives."

Fillers — In cosmetic and fragrance crafting, fillers add bulk or extend a product.

Fixative — A fixative stabilizes volatile oils and prevents them from evaporating too quickly. A common vegetable fixative is orris root. In soaps and bath products, the fixative can be the base soap, base oil, salts, or dried botanicals such as citrus peel.

Fragrance oil — A synthetically produced oil that reproduces the scent of a natural essential oil. The scents closest to the natural scent are the most successful in fragrance technology; it is no longer practical to extract the essence from many botanicals because of cost and scarcity. Other scents available include blends that do not exist in nature. Examples: "rain," "baby powder" oils.

Hand-milling — A method of making soap by grating a base soap, melting it with water, adding beneficial ingredients, and molding it to produce a superior quality soap.

Herb — The American Herb Society's official definition is "any plant that can be used for pleasure, fragrance, or physic." The term "herb" usually refers to a plant used for medicines, food, or fragrance that has soft stems and, after flowering, dies or withers to the ground. Example: basil. Some herbs are woody stemmed perennials that can grow to be small shrubs. Example: rosemary.

Hydrating — Maintaining or restoring normal fluid balance in the body or skin. Hydrating agents are used in cosmetics to keep the skin moist, firm, and young-looking. Examples: sweet orange oil, rose oil, chamomile.

Main scent — In fragrance crafting, this is the key scent. Other added scents modify and enhance the main scent to create a single blended theme. One scent alone has no staying power and does not make a perfume. The best fragrances are a result of artful combinations of scents.

Melt and pour — A method of creating handmade soap by melting a specially processed soap base in a microwave oven or a double boiler and pouring the melted soap base into a mold.

Potpourri — A fragrant mixture of dried herbs, flowers, and spices scented with fragrance oils in a vegetable fixative.

Refrigerant — A substance that cools inflammations and eases muscle pains. Example: menthol in mints.

Soap — The product of a chemical process called saponification in which an animal or vegetable fat and an alkali (lye) are combined, producing soap and glycerin.

Soap base — Soap made from fats and lye with no additives. Also refers to melt and pour soap before it is melted and additives are introduced.

Saponification — The chemical process in which soap is formed by combining fats or oils with an alkali (lye) to produce soap and glycerin.

Spice — A strongly flavored, aromatic substance usually obtained from the seeds, buds, or bark of a tropical plant. With a few exceptions, spices are not readily grown in home gardens in the northern hemisphere. Examples: cinnamon, cloves.

Stimulant — A substance that temporarily quickens the functional activity of the tissues. Example: using a luffa sponge stimulates circulation in the skin.

Superfatting — Adding extra oils and fats to a soap that will not be saponified, leaving the excess oils as a soothing moisturizer and creating a richer, milder soap. Superfatting can be done by adding oils to hand-milled soap or to a melt and pour soap base.

Synthetic — An artificially produced substance designed to imitate that which occurs naturally.

Volatile — Easily evaporated, such as an essential oil that has been extracted from the plant and no longer has the plant's cell structure to hold the scent. Adding a fixative stabilizes oils, reducing their volatility and helping them last longer. ❧

Cautions in Fragrance Crafting

When Using Essential Oils

Essential oils are highly concentrated and potent substances, and it is important to understand a few cautionary guidelines when crafting with them.

- Do not take essential oils internally.
- Avoid all essential oils, natural herbal products, and salt baths during pregnancy.
- Essential oils should always be used diluted in a base; they are not a perfume that can be applied directly to your skin.
- Keep essential oils out of reach of children.
- Do not allow essential oils to come into contact with plastic. Certain oils will dissolve some plastics.
- Keep essential oils away from varnished or painted surfaces. For example, cinnamon oil can cleanly strip paint from furniture.

When Using Botanical Additives and Ingredients

Just because plants are natural doesn't mean that they are safe. Many of the world's deadliest poisons come from plants. Herbs must be used with caution, as many are potentially dangerous irritants or can cause allergic reactions. Almost every additive, natural or synthetic, can trigger someone's allergy or irritate someone's sensitive skin.

Although these reactions are annoying, it is possible to avoid a recurrence by eliminating the offending ingredient. You can perform a simple skin test to make sure you aren't allergic to a soap by rubbing a small amount of soap and water on the tender area on the inside of your elbow. If you are sensitive to any ingredient, your skin will develop redness or a slight rash.

Here are some guidelines:

- Avoid using soaps with abrasive fillers on the face. Save those soaps for rough spots such as elbows, knees, and hands. Soaps made from melt and pour soap bases that include essential oils and extra fats for moisturizing are best to use to cleanse your face.
- For bath herbs, use the botanicals suggested. If you would like to explore this area further, there are many books available to educate you in the safe use of herbs.
- Use only herbs and flowers that are clean and free of insecticides and chemicals. Spray residues on plant material can irritate your skin. I prefer to use plants that I have grown myself. When this is not possible, purchase botanicals (ideally organically grown) from a natural food store or buy them fresh from the market and dry them yourself. Don't use dried botanicals from potpourri or dried flower arranging in bath products — these botanicals are not required to be food safe and may contain harmful dyes or chemicals.
- Cocoa butter, coconut oil, and almonds may produce a reaction in those allergic to chocolate and nuts.
- Natural emollients such as lanolin and glycerin may cause a reaction in those with sensitive skin.
- Honey, bee pollen, and beeswax may cause a reaction in those allergic to pollen. Do not use unpasteurized honey to scent products that will be used on infants.

General Soapmaking Cautions

- Be careful when working with melted soap. It can be very hot and can burn your skin if you spill it on you. Melt and pour soap bases are especially hot when melted (up to 190º F). If you do spill hot melted soap on you skin, place the exposed area in cold water immediately. Overheating the soap base in the microwave can cause the soap base to boil and overflow the cup and spill over on your hand. Heat the soap in brief intervals to prevent overheating. Keep melted soap away from children.
- Be careful when choosing plastic containers for molding your soaps. Some cannot take the high temperature of the melted soap and can melt and collapse, causing a spill.
- Spilled soap or oil can make floors slippery and cause dangerous falls. If you accidentally spill liquid soap or oil while working, clean it up immediately. The soap will solidify quickly — scrape it up and rinse the area well.
- Oils in baths can make the bathtub slippery, so take extra caution getting in and out of the tub.
- Clearly label any porous fragrance crafting tools, such as wooden spoons and plastic molds, so they won't be used in food preparation. Glass items are safe to use as they do not retain scents and residues.
- Clearly label your finished products with their contents and instructions for use. Some soaps look and smell so yummy that someone may mistake them for food!

MAKING MELT & POUR SOAP

Preparation Tips

- To calculate the amount of soap needed to fill your mold, fill the mold with water and pour into a measuring cup.

- Melt at least one extra ounce of soap to account for the soap that clings to the sides of the measuring cup.

- Slice and cut the soap base into small pieces for quick, easy melting.

- Be sure all the bowls, measuring cups and mixing spoons are completely dry. **Never add water** to melt and pour bases.

1. Place approximately 1 cup of soap pieces in a heat resistant glass measuring cup and microwave for 30 seconds to 1 minute on high. The amount of time needed for melting depends on the amount of soap. Melt the soap in small time intervals to keep it from boiling over.

2. Remove from the microwave and stir lightly to completely melt any remaining soap pieces. Do not leave the mixing spoon in the soap while heating in the microwave or when melting on the stove top.

Melting Option: You can also melt the soap in a double boiler on the stove. Adjust the heat to keep the soap at a constant liquid point. Do not let soap heat for more than 10 minutes.

3. Immediately add any additives or colorants to the melted soap and stir in gently to mix. If your soap has started to solidify at this time, you can gently reheat it to remelt it.

4. Add drops of fragrance oil until desired level of fragrance is achieved.

5. Pour the soap immediately into the mold after the fragrance has been added.

6. Let the soap cool and harden completely before removing from the mold. The soap will pop out easily when completely set.

Tips

- For a fast set, place the mold in the refrigerator until the soap is cooled.

- If your soap starts to solidify before you have poured it in the mold, gently reheat it to re-melt it.

- It is harmless to re-melt the soap. Repeated re-melting of clear glycerin soap base makes it more transparent as the excess moisture evaporates; repeated re-melting of coconut oil soap base makes a harder bar of soap.

- If you melt more soap than what fills your chosen mold, pour the leftover soap into another mold or plastic container, let set, unmold, and re-melt for another project. Always have an extra mold on hand in case this happens when you are creating your soaps.

- When cleaning up, don't put your measuring cups or spoons in the dishwasher. The soap is designed to make lots of luxurious bubbles, and the soap left on the equipment could foam and cause the dishwasher to leak. Roll up your sleeves and wash the equipment by hand.

Melt and Pour Techniques

Chunk Style Soaps

This double molded method suspends colored pieces of soap (soap #1) in a larger block of clear or opaque soap (soap #2). Soap #1 can be molded, slivered into long curls, cut into chunks, or grated before it is added to the mold and soap #2 is poured in. If soap #1 is made from the white glycerin base, it is best to chill the pieces before pouring the clear hot soap #2 on top of them to prevent the white pigment from leeching into the clear base. If soap #1 is made from white coconut oil soap base, don't chill it. Chilling could prevent the pieces from forming a solid bar. The creative possibilities are endless. An example of this style is the Plaid soap.

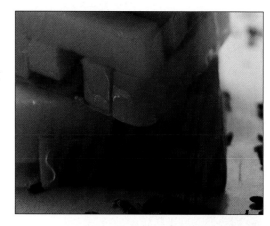

Defined Color Areas

You can create multi-colored soaps by double molding different colors and types of soap. For example, to make a checkered soap, you first mold soap in one color (soap #1), cut the soap into squares, and arrange the squares in the mold in a checkerboard pattern. The second color soap (soap #2) is poured on top. These soaps differ from chunk style soaps in that the pieces of soap #1 are arranged to create a specific pattern or motif. An example of this style is the Strawberry Soap.

Marbled

You can make beautiful marbled soaps by pouring clear glycerin and white glycerin soap bases into a mold at the same time and letting them gently swirl together. You can pour these soaps colored or not. You also can pour different colors of coconut oil base together for a marbled effect. You cannot, however, pour white coconut oil soap and clear glycerin soap together to create a marbled effect — they will separate because of their different densities. Examples of the marbling method are The Rock Crystal Soaps.

Layered

Since white coconut oil soap base and clear glycerin soap base separate when poured together because of their different densities, they are perfect for layering. The glycerin soap base sinks and the white coconut oil base rises to the top, with a mixed layer in-between. You also can layer different colors of the same soap base — simply let the first layer set before pouring on additional layers.

Additives on Top

Additives such as powdered spices, seeds, and grains tend to sink to the bottom of the mold, giving the soap a natural, whimsical look. To achieve this effect, simply add the additives to the melted soap just before pouring or place the additives in the bottom of the mold before pouring in the melted soap. Examples include Sea Mist Soap and Spa Soap.

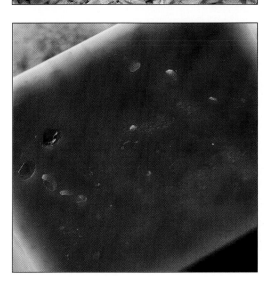

Additives Suspended

If you want the additives suspended throughout the soap, you need to do this extra step to keep them from sinking to the bottom. Add the additives to the melted soap base and gently stir with a fork to slowly cool and thicken the soap base. Immediately after the soap starts to thicken, pour the soap into the mold. The soap will harden with the additives suspended throughout the soap. Be careful to not let the soap thicken so much that it is too thick to pour. If this happens, re-melt and start again. I have found when mixing a large amount of the soap that it's helpful to have a pile of the same type of grated soap base on hand to add to the soap — this cools and thickens it quickly. Many of the loaf soaps are examples of this technique. ❧

MELT & POUR SOAP RECIPES

There are limitless techniques that can be used to create soaps with melt and pour bases. In this chapter, I have included easy and practical techniques that result in beautiful bars, then progress to more creative techniques — but just as easy to accomplish. Begin with easy molded soaps where you simply melt the base, add color and scent and pour it into a mold. Then progress to embedded surprises to create fun or fancy bars. Your friends and family will be delighted when you give them a bar with their initials on it. This is possible with the "Embossed Bars" technique in this chapter. But don't stop there — there are other exciting techniques in this chapter I am sure you will want to try.

**Ideas for wrapping and packaging your beautiful soaps
can be found in the section entitled, "Fragrance Collections."**

"We should all just smell well and enjoy ourselves more."
CARY GRANT

Easy Molded Soaps

It's never been easier to produce wonderful soaps at home. Melt and pour soap bases make creating fine, rich coconut oil based soaps and clear, fun glycerin soaps quick and easy. The soap base can be melted in a microwave oven and it cures almost immediately, so it's possible to create and package your own molded soaps in a single day. The following recipes show some of the creative options for making molded soaps.

Butter Bar

Shea butter and cocoa butter make this a moisturizing and softening soap. If you cannot find the buttery maple fragrance oil (a scent I could not resist), substitute a warm, yummy scent such as vanilla or a small amount of coconut fragrance.

Molds:
4 oz. rectangular soap mold
Flower soap mold (optional)

Cut up and melt:
4 oz. white coconut oil soap base

Add:
1 tablespoon shea butter
1 tablespoon cocoa butter
10 drops buttery maple fragrance oil
3 drops yellow liquid colorant

Pour melted soap into both molds. Let harden. Remove from the mold. Add a little melted soap to the molded flower to attach it to the bar soap. Package as shown. ❧

> *"Luxury need not have a price — comfort itself is a luxury."*
>
> GEOFFREY BEENE

Air Bar

Clear, clean citrus scents make this bar everyone's favorite.

Mold:
3 oz. rectangular soap mold

Cut up and melt:
3 oz. clear glycerin soap base

Add:
1/2 teaspoon .05 mica chips
5 drops bergamot oil fragrance oil
10 drops lemon oil fragrance oil

Stir the soap until it thickens so the mica is suspended throughout the soap. Pour in mold. Let harden. Remove from the mold and package as desired.

Water Bar

This soap has a soft, refreshing scent and a calming aqua tone.

Mold:
3 oz. rectangular soap mold

Cut up and melt:
3 oz. clear glycerin soap base

Add:
1 teaspoon .05 mica chips
10 drops ylang ylang fragrance oil

5 drops bergamot fragrance oil
2 drops blue liquid colorant
1 drop green liquid colorant

Stir the soap until it thickens so the mica is suspended throughout the soap. Pour in mold. Let harden. Remove from the mold and package as desired. ❧

Fire Bar

The warm, intense scents and colors of this soap stimulate your circulation and tone your skin.

Mold:
Two smaller molds for the chunks
3 oz. rectangular soap mold for the finished bar

Making the chunks

Cut up and melt:
3 oz. white glycerin soap base

Divide melted soap base into two containers. Use red and yellow liquid colorants to color one half orange and the other half yellow. Mold in the two small soap molds. Let harden. Unmold and slice into small pieces. Place the pieces in the 3 oz. rectangular mold. Place in the freezer to chill.

Making the bar

Cut up and melt:
3 oz. clear glycerin soap base

Add:
5 drops cinnamon fragrance oil
5 drops ginger fragrance oil
3 drops red liquid colorant

Mix in additives. Remove the mold from the freezer and pour the red melted clear soap base over the chilled colored pieces. Let harden. Remove from the mold and package as desired. ❧

Earth Bar

The nourishing wheat bran and cinnamon powder softly exfoliate the skin, leaving your body feeling smooth. The green parsley adds a touch of natural color. The scents are grounding and the moss green color reminds us of nature and the great outdoors.

Mold:
3 oz. rectangular soap mold.

Cut up and melt:
3 oz. white glycerin soap base

Mix and add:
4 drops green liquid colorant
2 drops orange liquid colorant
1/4 teaspoon wheat bran

1/4 teaspoon dried parsley flakes
A small sprinkle of cinnamon powder
10 drops pine fragrance oil
5 drops sandalwood fragrance oil
5 drops patchouli fragrance oil

Stir the soap until it thickens so the additives are suspended throughout the soap. Pour in the mold. Let harden. Remove from the mold and package as desired. ❧

Uplifting Soap

The lavender and peppermint are invigorating scents, but the melon tones it down to make a gentle, uplifting bar for calming frayed nerves. The small heart mold is a perfect shape, and the soft pink coloring is delicately rosy and restoring. This recipe makes three heart-shaped soaps.

Mold:
3 small heart-shaped molds, 2 oz. Pre-condition the molds with mold release.

Cut up and melt:
6 oz. white glycerin soap base

Add:
10 drops melon fragrance oil
5 drops lavender fragrance oil
5 drops peppermint fragrance oil
2 drops red liquid colorant

Pour in molds. Let harden. Remove from the molds and package as desired. ❧

Honey Soap

This energizing soap has a wonderful honey and floral fragrance and a lovely amber color. Honey softens the skin so it's great for extra thirsty complexions. Choose a clear soap base for clear bars or a whitened soap base for creamy-looking bars.

Mold:
3 oz. hexagonal bee mold to extend the theme. Because the honey softens the soap, pre-treat the mold with a mold release.

Cut up and melt:
3 oz. white glycerin soap base or clear glycerin soap base

Add:
1 tablespoon liquid honey
10 drops honey fragrance oil
5 drops honeysuckle fragrance oil
5 drops lavender fragrance oil
4 drops orange liquid colorant
1 drop black liquid colorant

Stir. Pour in the mold. Let harden. Remove from the mold and package as desired. ❧

Soap on a Rope

The fragrance blend is sweet and calming, reminiscent of a warm tropical evening — definitely one of my favorites. Use soft nylon cording for the rope (you'll need about 1 yd.) that will not disintegrate in the bath.

Mold:
Large conch shell soap mold

Cut up and melt:
6 oz. white coconut oil soap base

Add:
5 drops coconut fragrance oil

10 drops ylang ylang fragrance oil
5 drops vanilla fragrance oil

Knot the ends of the rope together to form a loop. Pour the scented soap into the mold. Immediately add the knotted end of the rope loop at the center of the mold. Let harden. Remove from the mold and package as desired. ❧

Mother of Pearl Shell Soaps

Dusting blue iridescent mica powder in the molds before pouring the melted soap gives these soaps a mother of pearl sheen. The clean, "white" scents make these soaps crisp and bracing.

Mold:

Shell tray mold designed for soaps. Brush blue iridescent mica powder inside the shell shapes with a soft, dry brush.

Cut up and melt:

4 oz. white coconut oil soap base (makes 2-3 shells)

Add:

5 drops peppermint fragrance oil

5 drops lavender fragrance oil

5 drops lily of the valley fragrance oil

Pour into the prepared molds. Let harden. Remove from the molds and package as desired. ❧

Pebble Soaps

The characteristic natural colors and forms of these pebble soaps have a naturally calming effect. The natural spices and herbs add color, texture, and a little scent.

Mold:
Molds for these soaps were made with latex rubber mold builder on smooth pebbles, 1-1/2" x 2".

Cut up and melt:
4 oz. white glycerin soap base (makes 3-4 soaps)

Add:
1/8 teaspoon each ground allspice, ground nutmeg, ground cinnamon, dried parsley flakes, wheat germ

10 drops amber fragrance oil

Optional: 3 drops black liquid colorant

Stir the soap until it thickens so the additives are suspended throughout the soap. Pour in molds. Let harden. Remove from the molds. ✿

Petal Soaps

These individual soaps are perfect for giving tender hands a quick, mild wash.
They can sit in a pretty jar or bowl beside the sink. The scent is delicate and gentle.

Mold:
The "molds" are silk rose petals — simply remove them from silk roses and trim them. The silk petal is thrown away after the soap is used.

Cut up and melt:
4 oz. clear glycerin soap base

Add:
5 drops rose fragrance oil

5 drops baby powder fragrance oil

Place the silk petals one by one in the melted soap base until the petal is coated. Remove the petal with a fork and place on a sheet of wax paper to set. Store the petals in an airtight plastic container if you're not using them right away to keep them fresh and prevent them from drying out. ❧

Loaf Style Soaps

These soaps are molded in plastic food containers or in rectangular metal candle molds. They create wonderful blocks of fragrant soap that are ready to be sliced and packaged for gift giving.

Spa Soap

This healing soap is filled with additives that nourish and exfoliate to rejuvenate and restore your healthy glow. The cleansing milk discourages wrinkles and won't clog pores.

Mold:
Plastic container 5" x 4" x 2-1/2" deep

Place in bottom of mold:
2 heaping tablespoons whole oatmeal
1 heaping tablespoon wheat bran

Cut up and melt:
24 oz. white glycerin soap base

Melt separately:
1 tablespoon shea butter

Mix shea butter thoroughly with 1 tablespoon powdered whole milk. Add to the melted soap base.

Add:
20 drops honeysuckle fragrance oil
10 drops clary sage fragrance oil
10 drops mango fragrance oil

Pour in prepared mold. Let harden. Remove from mold and slice into bars approximately 3/4" thick. Makes 6 bars.

"The sense of smell is the sense of imagination."

JEAN-JACQUES ROUSSEAU

Bread Loaf Soap

This soap is designed to look like a loaf of nourishing, natural bread. Someone once remarked that a soap I made looked like cheese. I developed this soap to complement it for a complete, well-balanced bath! The wheat bran and almond meal gently exfoliate the skin. The cinnamon lightly colors the soap and adds a warming, yummy scent.

Mold:
Metal candle mold 7-1/2" x 4" x 2-1/2" for this large-sized loaf. Be sure to pre-condition the mold with mold release.

Cut up and melt:
48 oz. white coconut oil soap base

Add:
2 tablespoons wheat bran
1 tablespoon almond meal
1/2 teaspoon powdered cinnamon
20 drops vanilla fragrance oil
15 drops cinnamon fragrance oil

Stir until the soap thickens so the additives stay suspended in the soap. Pour into pre-conditioned mold. Let harden. Remove from mold and rub 1 tablespoon powdered cinnamon on the outside of the loaf. Slice into bars approximately 5/8" thick. Makes 10 bars.

Citrus Honey Soap

The grains of bee pollen in this soap can help desensitize hay fever sufferers as they gently exfoliate the skin. The fragrance is cheering and refreshing.

Molds:

Plastic ice cube tray with small dome shapes for the light tan suspended shapes of the first molding

Plastic container 5" x 4" x 2-1/2" deep for the amber-colored loaf (second molding)

First Molding:

8 oz. white coconut oil soap base

10 drops honey fragrance oil

8 drops sandalwood fragrance oil

4 drops orange liquid colorant

2 drops black liquid colorant

Pre-condition the ice cube tray with petroleum jelly. Pour in the melted soap. Let harden. Unmold the small pieces and set aside.

Second Molding:

16 oz. clear glycerin soap

20 drops pink grapefruit fragrance oil

15 drops sweet orange fragrance oil

10 drops orange liquid colorant 3 drops black liquid colorants

Place the small dome shaped soap pieces from the first molding and 1 heaping tablespoon bee pollen in the mold. Pour in the fragrant, colored melted soap. Let harden. Remove from mold. Cut into slices 3/4" thick. Makes 6 bars.

Sea Mist Soap

This teal-colored soap is a good morning bar with an eye-opening fragrance. It's too harsh to use on your face, but your body will love it. The chunky sea salts help exfoliate and neutralize oils on the skin. The refreshing scent is long-lasting. Seaweed is a natural emollient and makes a lather like ocean froth.

Mold:
Plastic container 5" x 4" x 2-1/2" deep

Place in the mold:
1 tablespoon chunky sea salt
1/4 cup dried seaweed, ripped into small pieces

Cut up and melt:
24 oz. clear glycerin base

Add:
20 drops bergamot fragrance oil
10 drops mandarin fragrance oil
10 drops peppermint fragrance oil
10 drops blue liquid colorant
6 drops green liquid colorant

Pour the fragrant, colored melted soap into mold. Let harden. Remove from mold and cut into slices 3/4" thick. Makes 6 bars. ❧

Green Tea Soap

This cleansing soap is enchanting and sensual. The clean clear amber and muted green colors harmonize with the exotic scents.

Mold:
Metal candle mold 7-1/2" x 4" x 2-1/2". Be sure to pre-condition the mold with mold release.

Place in the mold:
1/4 cup green tea with jasmine blossoms

Cut up and melt:
48 oz. clear glycerin base

Add:
30 drops jasmine fragrance oil
15 drops ginger fragrance oil
20 drops green liquid colorant
6 drops black liquid colorant

Pour the fragrant, colored melted soap into the prepared mold. Let harden. Remove from mold. Cut into slices 5/8" thick. Makes 10 bars.

Embedded Surprises

Clear glycerin soaps can be embedded with small plastic toys, luffa sponges, fancy molded soaps, and good luck charms. These soaps make wonderful gifts and are lots of fun, but are unsafe for children under three years of age — the pieces are small enough to swallow.

Luffa Sponge Soap

The luffa sponge in these clear colored bars help to cleanse and stimulate your skin for a healthy glow.

Mold:
Round 2.5 oz. soap mold for each soap

Procedure:
Cut luffa sponge into 1" slices. Place one slice in each mold. Pour 2 oz. melted colored, scented clear glycerin soap base in the mold to cover and form the soap.

For Blue Luffa Soap: 2 drops blue liquid colorant, 6 drops ylang ylang fragrance oil

For Yellow Luffa Soap: 3 drops of yellow liquid colorant, 6 drops lemon fragrance oil
For Purple Luffa Soap: 2 drops red liquid colorant, 1 drop blue liquid colorant, 6 drops frankincense fragrance oil
For Green Luffa Soap: 2 drops green liquid, 1 drop yellow liquid colorant, 6 drops kiwi fragrance oil

Let harden. Unmold and package as desired. ❧

"To be overcome by the fragrance of flowers is a delectable form of defeat."

BEVERLY NICHOLS

Guardian Angel Soap

The soft, enjoyable fragrance of these bars invigorates, while the soap gently cleanses and moisturizes your skin. The molded angel in the clear soap base looks like a glass jewel. When using coconut oil soap base, which melts at a high temperature, there's no need to chill the angel soaps before pouring on the clear base.

Molds:
Angel motif tray mold for the angels
2 oval soap molds for the bars

First Molding:
White coconut oil soap base
Mold two white angels. Set aside to let harden.

Second Molding:
2 oz. clear glycerin soap base
5 drops orange fragrance oil

5 drops rose fragrance oil
3 drops pine fragrance oil
3 drops lemon fragrance oil

Pour the melted, scented clear soap base in the oval molds. Immediately place a white angel soap face down in each mold, slipping the angel soap in at an angle to prevent trapping air bubbles. Let harden. Unmold and package as desired. ❧

Good Fortune Soap

This energizing bar holds a Chinese coin that symbolizes prosperity and good luck. The celadon color is reminiscent of Chinese porcelains. Use a 2.5 oz. round soap mold.

Cut up and melt:
White coconut oil soap base

Add:
3 drops green liquid colorant
2 drops red liquid colorant
5 drops lavender fragrance oil
5 drops lime fragrance oil

Fill the mold three-quarters full with melted scented and colored soap. Let harden. Coat a Chinese coin with petroleum jelly (to keep it from tarnishing or discoloring the soap). Place the coin on the soap.

Cut up and melt:
1/2 oz. of clear glycerin soap base

Pour in mold over the coin. Let harden. Unmold and wrap. ✿

Embossed Soaps

Beautiful, embossed soaps that resemble expensive, luxury soaps from France are very easy to create with rubber stamps. I had my rubber stamps made at an office supply store, but you can also use purchased art stamps that have been cut from their mounts or purchase unmounted art stamps — ask for them at your local craft or rubber stamp store. Use rubber cement to temporarily glue the stamp into the bottom of the mold.

The stamp usually comes out with the soap when you unmold. To remove the stamp from the soap, stick a pin in the stamp and pull to remove, leaving a clear impression. The red rubber of the stamp sometimes colors the soap. To help prevent this, rub a small amount of petroleum jelly on the surface of the stamp before using the stamp in your soap molds.

Wipe out the residue of the rubber cement left in the mold with a paper towel before using the mold again.

Rose & Olive Soap

The olive oil adds a rich, moisturizing quality to this gray-green sensuous scented soap. The recipe makes two 3 oz. bars.

Mold:
Use oval soap molds. Glue a rubber stamp that says "Savon de Bain" (that's French for "bath soap") to the bottom of the mold.

Cut up and melt:
6 oz. white coconut oil soap base

Add:
1 tablespoon olive oil
10 drops rose fragrance oil
5 drops green liquid colorant
1 drop red liquid colorant

Pour soap in the mold over the glued-in-place motif. Let harden. Unmold.

Cardamom & Cinnamon Soap

The spices give the bar a beautiful, warm color. The classical motif rubber stamp and pear scent make a luxurious, extravagant bar. Makes two 4 oz. bars.

Mold:
Two 4 oz. plastic containers, glue the rubber stamp on the bottom.

Cut up and melt:
8 oz. white coconut oil soap base

Add:
1/2 teaspoon ground cinnamon
1/2 teaspoon ground cardamom
20 drops pear fragrance oil

Stir until the soap thickens so the additives stay suspended in the soap. Let harden. Unmold and package as desired. ❧

Examples of rubber stamps used for soap molding.

Double Molded Soaps

It's quick and easy to make molded melt and pour soaps, so you have endless creative opportunities for making beautifully crafted soaps. The following recipes show just a few techniques possible for double molding, cutting and remolding, and layering soap bases for unique bars.

Plaid Soap

This chunk style molded soap reflects the whimsical colors of a French country lavender field with the fresh scents of the garden.

Mold:
Four 4 oz. rectangular soap molds

First Molding:
12 oz. white glycerin soap base

For the light blue bar:
2 drops blue liquid colorant
6 drops violet fragrance oil

For the lavender bar:
1 drop blue liquid colorant
1 drop red liquid colorant
4 drops lavender fragrance oil

For the olive green bar:
2 drops green liquid colorant
1 drop orange liquid colorant
5 drops bergamot fragrance oil

Pour each color into a separate mold to make three bars. Let harden. Unmold. Slice each bar into long chunks. Make four bars of soap by placing chunks of varying colors into molds in two layers, with each layer perpendicular to one another. Place in freezer to chill.

Cut up and melt:
8 oz. clear soap base

Remove the molds from the freezer. Pour the melted clear soap over the chilled soap chunks. Let harden. Unmold and package as desired. ❧

> "*The world is a rose; smell it and pass it to your friends.*"
>
> PERSIAN PROVERB

Savon de bain

Flower Power Soaps

These soaps are large, sweet-smelling, colorful and powerfully fun! And you can create wonderful blooming colors.

Molds:

1-1/2" PVC pipe for flower centers, prepared with mold release and plastic wrap with a rubber band to hold one end closed.

Metal flower-shaped mold, treated with mold release.

First Molding:

4 oz. clear glycerin base
4 drops yellow liquid colorant
6 drops honey almond fragrance oil

Pour into the prepared pipe mold. Let harden. Unmold and set aside.

Second Molding:

12 oz. clear glycerin soap base
8 drops orange liquid colorant
20 drops sunflower fragrance oil

Place the molded tube of yellow soap into the center of the metal flower mold. Hold in place while you carefully pour the orange soap base around it. Let harden. Unmold and slice into three bars, each 3/4" thick. ✤

Strawberry Soaps

These whimsical, fruity scented soaps are joyful fun, and the added poppy seeds gently exfoliate your skin. Sweet and delicious, strawberries have long been used for their beauty benefits.

Molds:
Two 3 oz. oval soap molds to make 4 strawberry soaps

First Molding:
6 oz. clear glycerin soap base
1/4 teaspoon poppy seeds
10 drops strawberry fragrance oil
3 drops red liquid colorant

Stir the soap until thickened to suspend the seeds throughout the soap. Pour into mold. Let harden. Cut in half with a small sharp knife in a zig-zag pattern. Place one piece back in each mold.

Second Molding:
6 oz. clear glycerin soap base
10 drops kiwi fragrance oil
3 drops green liquid colorant

Press down the red molded piece in the mold to prevent the green soap from seeping under it while you carefully pour in the clear green soap base. Let harden. Unmold and trim off the top of the green to form the strawberry, using photo as a guide. Repeat with the remaining soap pieces. ❧

Rock Crystal Soaps

Clear crystals held supernatural powers with primitive people and were used for centuries to ward off evil spirits and to provide strength and were given as tokens of love and good luck. In the 17th century, ground precious stones were added to fragrant pomander mixtures with the belief that they would impart their mystical qualities to the blends.

It's easy to re-create the natural colors and shapes of semi-precious gems by cutting soaps into crystal shapes. The technique is the same for all the gems — just change the colors and the scents to create different types of crystal formations. I have included information about gemstones with many of the recipes that follow.

Basic Techniques for Rock Crystal Soaps

Molds: Use any mold that can be poured to a depth of approximately 2". A food container mold is a good shape to use. These soaps are simply marbled bars of soap that have been cut into crystal-shaped pieces.

For marbled soaps: Melt clear glycerin soap base and white glycerin soap base in different containers. The bases can be colored or left clear and white. Pour the melted soaps into the mold at the same time. Example: Malachite Soap.

For a chunk style soap in a marbled base: Mold scented and colored soap. Cut into crystal-shaped pieces 1/2" to 1". Place in the mold before pouring in the two melted soap bases to marbleize. Example: Milky Quartz Soap.

To create metallic veins through your soap: Brush a little metallic mica powder on the pieces before the second pouring. Example: Opal Agate Soap. Or brush on some powdered spices for a natural looking vein. Example: Jade Soap.

For layered looking gems: Pour melted clear glycerin soap base and melted white coconut oil base over the cut crystal-shaped pieces. Example: Amethyst Soap.

Cutting Soaps: The most important step is cutting the soaps after they are molded so they look like gems. Cut the soap into 2" to 3" pieces and trim by cutting random sharp, straight angles. This imitates the facets and clean cleavages of crystals.

Scenting: Use your favorite scents. Good choices include ylang ylang, amber, frankincense, cinnamon, and vanilla.

Opal agate soap

Milky quartz soap

Milky Quartz Soap

Sometimes milky quartz is mistaken for diamonds. It was symbolic of innocence and courage and was said to protect against evil spirits.

Mold clear glycerin soap base, allow to harden then cut into crystal shapes. Place pieces in another mold and pour in clear and white glycerin base to marbleize. Let harden, then unmold. Cut into crystal-shaped pieces.

Opal Agate Soap

Melt and mold clear glycerin soap base tinted with red colorant to make pink crystals. (Or use a variety of colors for the opal.) Cut into shapes. Brush copper and blue iridescent mica powder on the pieces. Place crystal pieces in mold.

Melt clear glycerin soap base and white glycerin base. Pour together over crystal pieces in mold to marbleize. Let harden. Unmold. Cut into crystal-shaped pieces.

Malachite Soap

Malachite symbolized courage and intelligence. Green gems were also a symbol of wealth.

Cut up and melt in separate containers, white glycerin soap base tinted with green colorant and clear glycerin soap base tinted with black colorant. Pour together into mold to marbleize.

Mix copper mica powder with a little glycerine and drop into mold and stir gently to distribute the mica through the soap. Let harden. Unmold. Cut into crystal-shaped pieces.

Jade Soap

Jade is a symbol of domestic bliss and success in love.

Melt and mold white glycerin soap base tinted with green liquid colorant and a tiny bit of black colorant to make a sage green color. Cut into pieces. Place pieces in the mold and brush with powdered cinnamon.

Melt, in separate containers, clear glycerin soap base and white glycerin soap base. Pour together over crystal pieces in mold to marbleize. Let harden. Unmold. Cut into crystal-shaped pieces.

Amethyst Soap

Amethyst symbolizes perfection, faithfulness, and sincerity. It's also believed to protect against drunkenness!

Melt in separate containers, clear glycerin soap base tinted with red and blue liquid colorants to make a lavender color and white coconut oil soap base. Pour together into mold to marbleize.

Rose Quartz Soap

Melt in separate containers, clear glycerin soap base and white glycerin soap base tinted with red colorant to make a pink color. Pour together in mold to marbleize. Mix Gold mica powder with a little glycerin and drop into mold. Stir gently to distribute the mica through the soap. Let harden. Unmold. Cut into crystal-shaped pieces.

Jade soap

Malachite soap

HAND MILLED
SOAP PROCEDURE

A gorgeous bar of hand-milled soap is pure luxury. Making it at home is easy and rewarding.

Preparation

Gather all the ingredients and measure all the additives. It is important to have all the ingredients ready to add so you don't have to leave the soap unattended on the stove or prepare the ingredients as the soap cools—it can become too thick to pour.

Prepare molds by applying a thin layer of mold release.

Note: Specific information on adding scents, colorants, and other ingredients is provided in the individual recipes. Remember to keep notes of ingredients and amounts used as you work for future reference.

1. Grate the soap into a bowl, using a hand kitchen grater. For a finer textured soap, further process the grated soap in a food processor. *See "Materials" section for information on soap bases to use.*

2. Place the grated soap in a heat resistant glass measuring bowl. Add any oil the recipe calls for. Add any water the recipe calls for.

3. Place the measuring bowl in a saucepan. Add about 2" of water into the saucepan. Place on the stove and turn the element to medium high. When the water begins to boil, turn down heat so water boils gently. Periodically mix the soap gently as it melts.

4. The soap will begin by clumping together. Use a wooden spoon to break up the clumps and incorporate the water into the soap. Be gentle so you won't make too many suds.

Second Stage of Melting:
As the soap continues to melt, the mixture will become smoother and look like watery cottage cheese. Continue to melt and stir the soap over the boiling water.

Third Stage of Melting:
In the final stage, the soap looks and acts like lumpy marshmallow cream. The soap will be stringy (this is called the "string" or "rope" stage) and all the water will be combined with the soap. This takes 10-15 minutes—don't worry if it takes a little longer. The soap *must* reach the string stage before you proceed. The mixture will quickly thicken.

You are now ready to take the soap out of the water bath and add the additional ingredients.

5. Working quickly, add any colorants and fragrance oils.

6. Add botanicals, oils, and any other ingredients the recipe calls for.

7. Stir the mixture thoroughly to disperse the ingredients.

8. Spoon the soap into the mold, tapping gently to remove any air bubbles. Let the soap harden in the mold.

9. The soap should be hard enough to unmold after four or five hours. If you are impatient to see your handmade soap, pop it into the freezer until frozen, then unmold. If the soap fails to harden after a few days (this can happen if it didn't reach the string stage), scoop it out, re-melt it, and re-mold. You can also salvage the batch by hand molding the soap into soap balls.

After unmolding, slice it into rounds or smaller pieces. Use a cardboard template to cut the soap into any shape you wish.

Let the soap dry and cure for up to three weeks. Keep turning the soap so it will not warp. Turning the soap is especially important in the first few days. ❧

HAND-MILLED SOAP RECIPES

Here are some of my tested recipes for creating luxurious hand-milled soaps. The technique is easy, yet it allows for abundant creativity. There is no limit to the types of additives, colors, or scents that can be combined to make a signature bar. Start with easy to make bath balls, then progress to rich and earthy Tuscany soap.

Bath Balls

The wheat germ, witch hazel, and rosemary in this soap help tone and nurture the skin; honey softens the skin so that it can absorb the moisturizing richness of the vitamin E. Hand-milled soaps are easy to hand form into balls. Melt and pour soap bases set up much too quickly to make successful soap balls.

Melt together:
2 cups processed, grated vegetable based soap
1/3 cup water
1/3 cup witch hazel

Add after the soap has melted:
1 tablespoon dried rosemary leaves
2 tablespoon wheat germ
Vitamine E oil, contents of 6 capsules
1 tablespoon liquid honey

5 drops tea tree oil
10 drops sweet orange fragrance oil
6 drops green liquid colorant, *optional*

Mix the additives, oils, and fragrances into the melted soap. Let cool. Hand mold into balls. Polish the balls with your hands and a few drops of orange oil to make them smooth. ❧

"There is no need to go to India or anywhere else to find peace. You will find that deep place of silence right in your room, your garden, or even your bathtub."

ELISABETH KUBLER-ROSS

Savon de Comte

This French-style "country soap" smells fabulous and exfoliates lightly while gently cleansing your skin for a clean, fresh feel. The extra oils, added for superfatting, make the bars rich and mild. A mounted rubber stamp was used to press a gilded fleur de lis motif in the curing bars.

Mold:
2-1/2" PVC pipe mold, prepared with mold release

Melt together:
2 cups processed, grated olive oil soap
1/2 cup water

Add and allow to melt:
1 tablespoon cocoa butter
1 tablespoon grated beeswax

Remove from heat and add:
1 tablespoon olive oil
10 drops sweet orange fragrance oil
5 drops lavender fragrance oil
5 drops lemon fragrance oil

Mix and pour in the prepared PVC mold. Let harden. When firm, unmold and slice into four bars, each 1" thick. Let cure for a few days. Dip the fleur de lis rubber stamp in copper mica powder and press into each bar to emboss. ❧

Zen Bar

Spices add lasting, harmonious aromas and mysterious impressions to this warming and calming bar. Use a 1 lb. soap mold.

Melt together:
2 cups processed, grated vegetable soap
1/2 cup water

Add after soap has melted:
1 teaspoon powdered cinnamon
1 teaspoon powdered star anise

10 drops sandalwood fragrance oil
5 drops cinnamon fragrance oil

Mix and pour into the prepared molds. When firm, unmold and cut into 4 bars. ❧

Tuscany Soap

The spices add rich, mellow scent and color, making this a luxurious bar with memories of a country excursion.

Mold:
Three 4 oz. rectangular soap molds, prepared with a mold release

Melt together:
2 cups processed, grated vegetable soap
1/2 cup water

Add after the soap has melted:
1/4 teaspoon cocoa powder
1 teaspoon cinnamon powder
1/4 teaspoon powdered cloves
10 drops cinnamon fragrance oil
10 drops bergamot fragrance oil
5 drops vanilla fragrance oil

Mix and pour in the prepared molds. Let harden. Unmold.

"Smell is a potent wizard that transplants us across thousands of miles and all the years we have lived."

HELEN KELLER

BATH SALTS

Bath salts are easy to mix, making them an ideal project to do with children. Measuring and counting the fragrance and coloring drops can be educational and fun. Salts can be found at supermarkets and drugstores and can be produced at home for a fraction of the cost of store-bought products.

The base of bath salts neutralizes the acids on the skin so the fragrance will cling to the body. The scents are soothing, and Epsom salts relax and heal your skin. The salts also act as an effective fixative to hold the scents. Several recipes are included, as well as the technique for the popular solid fizzing bath salts.

Most of the cost of purchased bath salts is for packaging, so the presentation of your bath salts is just as important as the salts themselves to the finished product.

Pictured top row, left to right: baking soda, coarse salt, Epsom salt. Second row, left to right: buttermilk powder, chunk sea salt, fine sea salt.

Ingredients

Use these ingredients for making your own bath salts and solid fizzing bath salts.

Baking soda (Sodium bicarbonate) is a mild alkaline salt used in bath salt formulas offering soothing and softening qualities. It is also a good salt base for absorbing fragrances; when the salts hit the hot water of the bath they release the scents for a pleasant, fragrant soak.

Citric acid is a preservative obtained by fermenting citrus fruit sugars. It is used along with baking soda to create fizzy bath salts. Citric acid is highly astringent and a great toner for the skin. You can find citric acid at stores that sell winemaking supplies and at health food stores.

Coarse salt can be used as the base for fragrant bath salts. I prefer to get the large, chunky crystals from the health food store for the most attractive salts. The salts neutralize your skin so the fragrant oils cling and make your skin smell beautiful for hours. Salt is also healing and soothing for your skin.

Cornstarch is used in the solid, fizzy "bath bombs" as a filler and binder. It's also an absorbent ingredient in the scented powder recipe.

Epsom salts are mild alkaline salts that disperse easily in water. They are excellent in bath salt blends for soothing skin inflammations and muscular aches. Use Epsom salts alone with added fragrance oils or mix with other salts to create different blends. The fine texture and sparkle make Epsom salts very attractive when packaged in fancy clear bottles.

Powdered buttermilk is a nice addition to bath salts that helps cleanse, soften, and nourish the skin. It is easily absorbed and a very luxurious addition to your bath water.

Sea salt is an excellent salt base for fragrant bath salts when a fine, granular salt is preferred. Sea salts also can be found in coarse and chunky crystalline forms. You may be able to find salts from the Dead Sea at health food stores — Dead Sea salts are famous for their curative properties.

Rose water is a soothing, emollient liquid with a gentle rose fragrance. It is made of a solution of pure essential rose oil and distilled water. It can be used instead of water in hand-milled soap recipes and for solid bath salts for added scent and softening properties.

Witch hazel is a low growing shrub (*Hamamelis virginiana*) with fragrant blossoms. The distillation of the leaves and bark produces a clear liquid. It is a remarkably effective astringent that is soothing and healing. Use instead of water in the preparation of the solid bath salts.

Basic Instructions for Creating Bath Salts

1. Place the measured salts in a large bowl and mix well.
2. Take out about 1/2 cup in a small bowl. Add the drops of fragrance and coloring to this smaller amount and mix well. Add the blended mixture to the large bowl, a little at a time until you are pleased with the color strength. Pour your salts in a glass jar with a tight fitting lid. Store and shake every day for one week before packaging.

To use: Draw a warm bath and add 1/4 cup of the fragrant salts to the running water. Hop in and relax, inhaling deeply to experience the soothing aromas.

Seashore Salt Rub

These salts are designed to rub on your skin while you stand in the tub before a cleansing shower. Salt tones and exfoliates the skin. Kelp is a natural cleanser and moisturizer that helps color the salts to look like beach sand. Kelp adds a wonderful sea scent, but beware — adding too much kelp powder will make the salt rub smell too strongly of the outgoing tide! The other fragrances make the blend smell sweet and refreshing.

Mix together following Basic Instructions:
1 cup Epsom salts
1 cup sea salt
1 teaspoon Atlantic kelp powder
1 tablespoon glycerin
15 drops peppermint fragrance oil
10 drops mulberry fragrance oil

Shake every day for a week. Package as desired. ❧

Shimmering Body Soak Crystals

These have a wonderfully refreshing and restorative fragrance and a sparkling gleam.

Mix together following the Basic Instructions:

2 cups Epsom salts

2 tablespoons glycerin

1 teaspoon white pearl mica powder

10 drops tangerine fragrance oil

5 drops lime fragrance oil

5 drops peppermint fragrance oil

5 drops grapefruit fragrance oil

Shake every day for a week. Package as desired.

Buttermilk Bath Salts

Classic beauties like Cleopatra and Mary Queen of Scots made milk baths famous. These sumptuous salts make your skin feel soft and silky. The cake bake fragrance adds an appetizing aroma, but can be omitted.

Mix together following the Basic Instructions:

1 cup buttermilk powder

1 cup sea salt

10 drops vanilla fragrance oil

5 drops honey fragrance oil

5 drops cake bake fragrance oil

Shake every day for a week. Package as desired. ❧

Lavender Bath Salts

The legendary allure of lavender and rose come together in these perfumed salts that contain glycerin for extra moisturizing. Crushing the lavender buds prevents the fragrant buds from clogging your drain — and they will float on the surface of your bath water. The soft lavender color looks beautiful in a bottle.

Mix together following the Basic Instructions:

2 cups Epsom salts
1 cup baking soda
1/2 cup dried lavender buds, crushed
2 tablespoons glycerin
10 drops lavender fragrance oil
5 drops Victorian rose fragrance oil
5 drops red liquid colorant
3 drops blue liquid colorant

Shake these salts every day for a week to keep them from clumping together and forming a solid mass. Package as desired. *Option:* Omit the crushed lavender and add 10 extra drops of lavender oil. ❧

Vanilla Bean Bath Salts

Vanilla is a rich, warm scent that leaves a lavish impression. Place a whole vanilla bean pod in the jar for added interest.

Mix together following the Basic Instructions:

1 cup Epsom salts
1 cup sea salt
20 drops vanilla fragrance oil
4 drops musk fragrance oil
4 drops yellow liquid colorant
2 drops black liquid colorant

Split open the long pods of two vanilla beans and scrape out the small, fragrant seeds that hold most of the fragrance. Mix with the salts. Shake every day for a week. Package as desired. *Option:* Chop the pod finely and mix in for additional color. ❧

Foaming Bath Salts

These salts are added to the rush of water as you fill your bath for a delightfully foamy and aromatic bath. They are wonderful for softening hard water.

Mix together following the Basic Instructions:
1 cup coarse salt
1 cup grated soap
1 cup Epsom salts
5 drops honeysuckle fragrance oil
5 drops honey fragrance oil
3 drops lily of the valley fragrance oil
5 drops yellow liquid colorant

Shake every day for a week. Package as desired. 🐝

Solid Fizzing Bath Salts

Follow these steps to create your own solid fizzing bath salts. After you master these simple steps, you will be able to produce solid bath salts very quickly. Choose deep molds with large details. No mold pre-treatment is necessary.

Basic Instructions for Solid Fizzing Bath Salts

1. Assemble the salts and mix well in a large bowl.

2. Remove a small amount of the mixed salts to another bowl. Add the fragrances, colorants, and other additives called for in the recipe. Blend well. Add back into the large bowl of salts and mix.

3. Remove approximately 1/3 of the blended, colored salts to a smaller bowl.

4. Spritz this small amount lightly with a fine mist of the liquid specified in the recipe. Do not over mist or your bath salts will start to fizz! The salts need to just be damp enough to hold together. With your hands (so you can judge the amount of dampness), mix the salts well. If needed, mist again and mix.

5. Pack the damp salts into a mold. Press down hard to pack the salts in, adding more if needed. Pack only one mold at a time.

6. Place a piece of thin cardboard over the mold and flip over. The solid bath form will fall out. Be gentle!

7. Carefully slide the molded salt form to a board or cookie sheet covered with wax paper.

8. Leave the salts to dry overnight to a hard, dry "bath bomb."

9. To use: Draw a warm bath and drop the solid bath salt into the water. Hop in and let the salts dissolve and fizz away stress and tension. (You can't take the solid bath salt out when it's halfway dissolved — all the fizzing action has been used up!) Inhale deeply to experience the soothing aromas.

Tips

- If your molded salt breaks at any time, just re-mold.
- If your salts seem to "grow" and puff out, you have added too much water! Take the salts, place them back in the small bowl and mix in some dry salts to stop the fizzing action. Remold.

- If you want to use only a part of the molded salts, place in a bag and break with a hammer. (They're hard!) Place a piece in the bath.

"Nothing awakens a reminiscence like an odor."

VICTOR HUGO

Fizzy Bath Heart

The rosy scent with the spicy clove note gently relieves fatigue and tension while you enjoy a quiet soak. Use a heart shaped soap mold.

Mix according to Basic Instructions:

1 cup baking soda
1/2 cup citric acid
1/4 cup cornstarch
10 drops rose fragrance oil

5 drops clove fragrance oil
4 drops red liquid colorant

Spray with rose water. Mold. Unmold. Package as desired. 🌿

Effervescent Bath Tablets

These tablets are designed to compliment the Elements Soaps (Air, Water, Fire, Earth) and have embossed motifs. They are easy to blend and were molded in 2 oz. rectangular soap molds with a rubber stamp motif (with the word "Air," "Water," "Fire," and "Earth") glued into bottom of each mold.

Basic Tablet Recipe

(Makes two 2 oz. tablets)
1 cup baking soda
3/4 cup citric acid

Follow the Basic Instructions for mixing and molding Solid Fizzing Bath salts.

Air Bath Tablet

Invigorating and calming, with sky blue coloring and the scent of rain.

To the Basic Tablet Recipe, add:
20 drops rain fragrance oil
2 drops blue liquid colorant

Spray the salt mixture with witch hazel before molding.

Earth Bath Tablet

Relaxing and stress relieving, with a moss green color, brown speckles, and earthy scent.

To the Basic Tablet Recipe, add:
20 drops sandalwood fragrance oil
3 drops green liquid colorant
1 drop red liquid colorant
1/2 teaspoon cinnamon powder

Spray the salt mixture with rose water before molding.

Water Bath Tablet

A refreshing wake-up with bracing scents and a deep aqua color.

To the Basic Tablet Recipe, add:
10 drops peppermint fragrance oil
10 drops bayberry fragrance oil
5 drops green liquid colorant
3 drops blue liquid colorant

Spray the salt mixture with witch hazel before molding.

Fire Bath Tablet

Warming and sensuous, with a rich orange color and spicy orange scent.

To the Basic Tablet Recipe, add:
5 drops cinnamon fragrance oil
10 drops sweet orange fragrance oil
4 drops orange liquid colorant

Spray the salt mixture with witch hazel before molding.

> *"A perfume is more than an extraction; it is a presence in abstraction."*
>
> GIORGIO ARMANI

Chocolate Tub Truffles

Sweet and comforting for when you need extra pampering without the calories.

Mix together following Basic Instructions:
1 cup baking powder
3/4 cup citric acid
1/4 cup cornstarch

Add and mix well:
1/4 cup finely grated cocoa butter
1 teaspoon cinnamon powder

1 teaspoon cocoa powder
1 tablespoon chocolate candy sprinkles
20 drops chocolate fragrance oil
10 drops vanilla fragrance oil

Spray salt mixture with witch hazel. Hand mold
into small (1-1/2" diameter) balls. Let dry.

Spiced Chai Bath Bombs

These are supercharged for extra fizzing action. The warming scents bring inner peace and fizz away stress and tense muscles.

Mold:
4 oz. dome mold

Mix together following Basic Instructions:
1 cup baking soda
1 cup citric acid
1/4 cup cornstarch

Add and mix well:
1 teaspoon each powdered clove, powdered cinnamon, powdered star anise, and powdered cardamom
20 drops vanilla fragrance oil

Spray salt mixture with witch hazel. Place a few whole spices in the bottom of the mold before molding. ❧

BOTANICAL BLENDS

Plants provide us with shelter, utensils, fragrance, medicine, and flavor. They have proved beneficial to health and have enhanced humans' natural beauty since the very earliest times. The domestic and cosmetic use of herbs is varied — we use them to make soaps, bath products, and fragrances. They reward us with a superior product and the activity of creating.

Some of the sweetest scents in the world are plant smells. They add aroma to fragrance crafting, and most have specific attributes as beauty aids. The list presented here is only a very small sampling of the botanicals available. I chose them because they are the easiest to find or grow, have beautiful perfume, and are especially effective. Find these ingredients in health food stores or fresh at the market or grow your own. Choose pesticide-free, organically grown fruits and herbs.

CAUTION: Because some plants are irritants and potentially dangerous, please restrict your use of botanicals to this selection of commonly found or grown herbs if you are just discovering natural, homemade beauty products.

Botanicals to Use in Fragrance Crafting

Chamomile — Both the Roman chamomile (*Chamaemelum nobile*) and German chamomile (*Matricaria chaomilla*) are fragrant and useful. Chamomile has a delicious, apple-pineapple fragrance that is fresh and soothing.

Citrus peel — Whole, cut, or powdered peels of oranges, limes, lemons, and grapefruit are useful and fragrant additions to your recipes. The dried peel is used as a fixative in bath herb blends to help to enhance and hold the scents. The fresh scents of citrus are energizing, stimulating, and uplifting.

Green tea — Green teas are made from the leaves of the *Camellia sinensis* bush that are picked and dried. Green tea is linked to a number of health benefits — not only from drinking it but also from experiencing its exhilarating and rejuvenating fragrance.

Lavender is the most popular fragrance crafting herb. Its Latin name, *lavare*, means "to wash". This evergreen plant with purple flowers was used by the ancients for its relaxing and soothing qualities and its antiseptic and healing characteristics. Its bright, strong floral fragrance is the backbone of many perfumes. Lavender can be used in soap formulas or as a bath herb.

Lemon verbena (*Aloysia triphylla*) has an excellent floral-lemon scent that is delicate and stimulating. The long fragrant leaves are a favorite addition to soap recipes and bath herb blends. Lemon verbena is found in health food stores. (It makes a wonderful, calming tea.) Lemon balm can be used in place of lemon verbena.

Mints — The refreshing scents of mints are stimulating additions to all your bath preparations. I prefer peppermint (*Mentha piperita*) for fragrance crafting. It has a strong, fresh scent and is high in menthol, which is cooling. Mint is also an excellent antiseptic. Mints are extremely easy to grow — in fact, many gardeners consider them invasive and hard to control.

Pictured: Orris root and pine. Other botanicals that can be used are pictured in the "Materials" section.

Orris root is the dried rhizome of the iris plant. Historically, it was widely used as a vegetable fixative for cosmetic products. It no longer is used commercially because many people are allergic to it. It is, however, excellent for holding scent in sachets and potpourri blends.

Pine — Needles from the balsam fir and grand fir are the most aromatic. They are purifying and calming when added to bath preparations. The scent is refreshing and reviving. Use cautiously — some people are allergic to pine.

Rosemary — Dried, whole rosemary is stimulating, soothing, and uplifting.

Sage — The name sage is from the Latin *salvere*, meaning "to be in good health." It is an important herb for its antiseptic, astringent, and healing properties. Its strong scent is relaxing, stimulating, and uplifting. Its healing qualities aid problem skins when used in bath bags and soap recipes.

Basic Bath Herb Recipe

To blend: Place the dried botanicals listed in a bowl and mix.
To use: Place 1/4 cup of the blend in a muslin bag. Simmer the bag in a pan on top of the stove with one quart of water for 10 minutes to make a fragrant "tea." Pour the tea along with the bag into your bath water and relax. Use the wet bag to scrub and stimulate your skin. Discard after use.

Sachets and Potpourri

Gentle fragrance blends tucked into the folds of stored linens or displayed in a fancy bowl are some of life's little pleasures. The scents have a positive effect on our moods.

To make sachet blends, gently mix ingredients listed in recipes. For potpourri, add the fragrant oils to the fixative before blending with the dried botanicals. ❧

Spa Bath Herbs

These are subtly aromatic, with hints of fresh flowers and citrus. This blend lifts spirits and leaves skin clean and fresh smelling.

Recipe:
1 cup dried whole lemon verbena leaves
1/2 cup dried lavender buds
1/2 cup dried whole chamomile flowers
1/4 cup dried orange peel

Green Tub Tea

Recipe:
1/2 cup green tea
1/3 cup dried whole balsam pine needles
1/4 cup dried whole rosemary needles
1/4 cup dried lavender buds ❧

Lavender Linen Sachets

This gently scents linens and helps discourage insects.

Recipe:
1/2 cup dried lavender buds
1/4 cup whole peppercorns
2 tablespoons broken cinnamon sticks
1 tablespoon whole cloves

Mix herbs and package in little cloth "pillows." ❧

Scented Sea Glass Potpourri

The porous, frosted glass pieces hold the fragrance for this odoriferous, sparkling display. Find pieces of tumbled glass with mosaic supplies in craft stores.

Recipe:
1/4 cup sea glass
10 to 15 drops bayberry fragrance oil

Mix glass and fragrance oil. Display in a shell or a basket. Refresh with additional oil as needed. ❧

Spicy Pear Potpourri

A richly aromatic and spicy potpourri for a courtly display. Orris root is used as a fixative.

Recipe:
1/2 cup whole star anise
1/2 cup broken cinnamon sticks
3/4 cup whole cloves
1 tablespoon whole allspice
2 tablespoons whole rose hips
1 tablespoon orris root, chunk style
1 tablespoon brandy
20 drops pear fragrance oil

Mix together. *To refresh your blend*, sprinkle potpourri with brandy and mix well. The alcohol will renew the fragrance.

Optional: Add clove-studded pear pomanders to decorate.

"It is believing in roses that one brings them to bloom."

FRENCH PROVERB

BUBBLE BATH

You can find liquid glycerin soap in the fragrance crafting departments of craft stores. It is unscented and formulated for creating your own quality bubble bath blends, fragrant blowing bubbles, shampoos, and fragrant hand soaps. (It's a new product — you may need to ask for it.)

Baby Bubbles

This is a gentle bubble bath for baby or mom. The built-in wand is great for blowing bubbles.

Gently mix until blended:
1 cup liquid glycerin soap
1 tablespoon glycerin
10 drops rose fragrance oil
10 drops baby powder fragrance oil
1 drop red liquid coloring

Pour into decorative bottles. Make the bubble wand by twisting brass wire and adding glass beads. Insert the end in the cork bottle stopper and glue to secure. ❧

"Smells are surer than sounds and sights to make the heartstrings crack."

RUDYARD KIPLING

Rose Bubble Bath

Who can resist the fragrance of roses?

Gently mix until blended:
1 cup liquid glycerin soap
1 tablespoon glycerin
15 drops rose fragrance oil

2 drops red liquid coloring

Pour into decorative bottles. Seal with a cork. ❧

Sea Bubbles Foaming Bath Oil

This foaming, stimulating oil has a refreshing, herbal fragrance and is great for those with dry skin or hard water. The mixture will separate in the bottle, creating an appealing layered blend — simply shake before adding to your bath.

Gently mix until blended:

1/2 cup liquid glycerin soap
2 drops blue coloring
1 tablespoon glycerin
1/4 cup sweet almond oil
20 drops spearmint fragrance oil

10 drops cucumber fragrance oil
6 drops sage fragrance oil
1/2 teaspoon white pearl mica powder

Pour into decorative bottles. Decorate the cork stopper with a small seashell. ❧

BATH & MASSAGE OILS

Bath oils pamper your skin and help soften hard water. They envelop you with a fine film of oil that will soften and scent your skin as the fragrance rises in the steam, perfuming the air. They are beautiful to display in the bathroom.

Because homemade bath oils do not contain preservatives, they can become rancid after a few months. Adding vitamin E, a natural preservative, helps bath oils last longer and adds healing properties.

Oils to Use in Bath Oil Blends

In bath and massage oils, the base oils carry and dilute the concentrated essential oils used to scent them. The base oils also inhibit evaporation (acting as fixatives) and are quickly absorbed into the skin.

Almond Oil (*Prunus communis*) is the finest and best all-purpose carrier oil. It is neutral, has no scent, and is non-allergenic. It is easily absorbed into the skin where it nourishes and moisturizes. Sweet almond oil (var. *dulcis*), the variety of almond that produces the nuts we eat, is superior to almond oil, but a great deal more expensive. Look for pure pressed oil that has been extracted without the use of chemical solvents.

Baby oil from the pharmacy is a delicate, soothing, and very gentle oil that imparts its soft fragrance when used as a base for bath oils. I like to use it with floral blends for a soft, romantic oil.

Olive oil — A very fine, strongly scented rich oil that is very good for sensitive skin. Use cold pressed, extra-virgin olive oil. It is useful as a healing and soothing bath oil when blended with other base oils.

Sunflower oil has many of the same qualities as safflower oil and is less expensive. It naturally contains vitamin E and so has a slightly longer shelf life than safflower oil. This less expensive oil, when blended with higher quality oils, acts as a filler.

Vitamin E oil — is an exceptional antioxidant and natural preservative in fragrant bath oils where botanicals have been added for decoration. Vitamin E can be found in capsule or liquid form; capsules are less expensive. Simply cut or pierce the capsule and squeeze out the oil.

Basic Instructions for Blending Bath Oils

1. Blend all the oils and fragrances together.

2. Place in a glass container with a tight fitting lid and shake or stir every day for a week. This helps the fragrances blend and allows you to make adjustments.

3. Add the coloring and bottle. Many items can be placed in the bottle before pouring in the oil to add a wonderful decorative touch, such as botanicals, silk flowers, and oil bath beads. Make sure botanicals are completely dry — fresh items will mold and make your oil rancid.

Baby Massage Oil

Do not add oil to the bath water when bathing a baby; it makes them too slippery! This gentle oil is for massaging your baby after the bath. In aromatherapy, chamomile is used to foster patience and take away worries, so this scent can help a new mom relax. Remember Peter Rabbit's mother recommended chamomile tea after harrowing escapes from the cabbage patch!

Mix following Basic Instructions:
1 cup sweet almond oil or 1 cup baby oil
20 drops chamomile fragrance oil
10 drops rose fragrance oil

Accent the bottle with silk rosebud. 🌹

Lavender Bath Oil

The olive oil adds a strong aroma that blends well with the lavender and rose to make this a rustic but luxurious bath oil.

Mix following Basic Instructions:
1 cup olive oil
1/2 cup almond oil
30 drops lavender fragrance oil
20 drops rose fragrance oil

Add a few dried lavender buds or rosebuds to the bottle. ❧

Botanical Bath Oil

This sweet-smelling blend soothes and nourishes. The sunflower oil is inexpensive, making this oil economical for gifts. The light amber color underscores the honey fragrance.

Mix following Basic Instructions:
1/2 cup almond oil
1/2 cup sunflower oil
Oil from 10 pierced vitamin E capsules
20 drops sunflower fragrance oil
10 drops honey fragrance oil

Add:
3 drops orange Liquid colorant
1 drop black liquid colorant

Accent the cork with a small wooden honeybee.

BATH POWDER RECIPES

Blend the fragrance oils and added oils well with the powders in a large bowl to create these soothing blends.

Soothing Baby Powder

This healing blend soothes inflamed skin and is gentle enough for a new baby. The warm sweet scent of chamomile is calming and relaxing.

Ingredients:

1/2 cup cornstarch
2 tablespoons dried chamomile blossoms, ground and sifted through a fine sieve
10 drops chamomile fragrance oil ❧

Queen Bee Dusting Powder

The added oil in this powder blend makes it soothing and soft. The French clay absorbs oil. The fresh, sweet floral fragrance will make you feel like royalty!

Ingredients:
3/4 cup cornstarch
1 tablespoon French clay
1/2 cup rice flour
1 tablespoon sweet almond oil
20 drops neroli fragrance oil

FRAGRANCE COLLECTIONS

Now that you are practiced in making soap, bath salts, and bubble bath — it is time to put all your knowledge together to create luxurious and creative collections. On the following pages, collections of fragrance products are presented as examples. Use your own creativity to create themed collections for family and friends.

Recipes for each of the products shown in the collections can be found in previous chapters.

Packaging Fragrance Crafted Projects

When you have taken the time to create beautiful fragrance gifts, presenting them attractively is equally important. A useful tip for creating gift packages is to follow a theme for your gift presentation — choose products that are linked by shape, color, or fragrance or pick a theme that reflects the recipient's favorite hobby or interest to create a unique, personalized package.

Packaging Tips

- Packaging should accent the designs of your soaps without overpowering them. Simple, minimal designs are best. Use coordinating creative accents.

- Melt and pour soaps should be wrapped in plastic wrap to keep the soap fresh and the fragrance from dispersing. The soap can develop white crystals on the surface if it dries out. These crystals are harmless but unsightly. They are often the result of using fragrance oils that have been diluted with alcohol.

- Let hand-milled soaps dry completely before packaging. They don't need to be covered with plastic wrap — they actually benefit from being unwrapped, as they will continue to harden. Packaging that is not airtight, such as paper, works best.

- **Always** label your soap and fragrance products, listing all ingredients. Add instructions for use where applicable.

- Store soaps and bath products out of direct light in a cool, dry place. ❧

Elements Collection

These small gift packages reflect our emotional responses to color and scent: "Air" is uplifting and fresh, "Water" is head clearing and promotes well being and alertness, "Fire" is passionate and invigorating, and "Earth" is balancing, relaxing, and peaceful.

The four soaps (recipes on pages 36-39) are packaged with coordinating Effervescent Bath Tablets (recipes on pages 86,87) in crisp clear cellophane bags. Tie the bags shut and choose tags that reflect the element's theme — a feather for "Air," raffia and a leaf for "Earth," a seashell for "Water," gold metallic ties for "Fire."

Spa Collection

This rejuvenating collection of fragrant bath products features all the benefits of a spa experience at home. The packaging uses neutral natural colors that are comforting and soothing.

The Soaps

- Spa Soap, wrapped in raffia cloth and accented with a button
- Luffa Sponge Soap, wrapped in raffia cloth and tied with natural raffia
- Bath Balls in a see-through drawstring bag

Fragrant Companions

- Shimmering Body Soak Crystals in a glass jar with a wooden scoop
- Spa Bath Herbs in parchment envelopes

Finishing Touches

Other additions could include a rubber ducky, a wooden foot roller, or a natural exfoliant (a sea sponge, a bath brush, or sisal washcloth). To involve all the senses, add herbal tea bags, fragrant candles, and a nature sounds tape. ❧

Spa Bar

BATH
HERBS

Gentle Baby Collection

This nurturing package is for both mom and baby (happy mom = happy baby, and vice versa). The soothing scents of chamomile will help baby sleep better, so mom will, too. Pamper the delicate skin of an infant with gentle herbal powder, massage oil, and soothing soaps. The soft pinks and frothy whites can be changed to pale icy blues or soft creamy yellows.

All the products were accented with frothy tulle bows and silk roses. Silk rose petals were used for labels (you can write on them with a permanent marker).

The Soaps

- Uplifting Soap, first wrapped in plastic wrap, then in tulle, gathered at the top with a bow
- Guardian Angel Soap is gentle and lovely for mother or child
- Petal Soaps in a frosted glass bowl will make mom feel special and indulged

Fragrant Companions

- Fizzy Bath Heart in a frosted paper gift bag
- Baby Bubbles in a heart-shaped glass bottle with a built in wire bubble wand
- Baby Massage Oil in a frosted glass bottle
- Soothing Baby Powder in a glass jar

Finishing Touches

Other additions could include a pacifier, a rattle, or a stuffed toy.

Picnic Basket

Here is a tasteful assortment of soaps and bath products with a fun food theme. Be sure to include some actual edibles: delectable pastries, rich dark chocolates, colorful fresh fruit. The blue checks in the packaging are cheery and restful.

The Soaps

- Bread Loaf Soap wrapped in plastic with a paper label
- Butter Bar wrapped in glassine paper and tied with raffia
- Strawberry Soap in a berry basket with excelsior filler

Fragrant Companions

- Buttermilk Bath Salts in an old-fashioned soda glass with a scoop
- Chocolate Tub Truffles in a glass candy jar ❧

Oceans Collection

Thalassotherapy is a spa therapy that uses ocean products such as seaweed and sea salt. Bringing the ocean into our homes helps stimulate our senses and reminds us of our place in the universe. The Seashore Salt Scrub brings natural moisturizers to your bath, and the Sea Mist Soap stimulates the skin as it cleanses and scents the air with the smell of the sea. The greens and blues remind us of water and the sea and are calming and invigorating.

The Soaps

- Sea Mist Soap has a raffia cloth wrapper and a seashell as a label
- Soap on a Rope is the perfect accompaniment (and men will love it)
- Mother of Pearl Shell Soaps to add glistening reflections to the collection

Fragrant Companions

- Seashore Salt Rub in a blue glass bowl with a shell for a scoop
- Sea Bubbles Foaming Bath Oil in a bottle with a shell on the cork and a shell for a tag
- Scented Sea Glass Potpourri displayed in a shell. This can be wrapped in plastic wrap when presenting as a gift.

Honeybee Collection

The word "honey" comes from ancient Hebrew and means "enchant." Made by bees from the nectar of flowers, honey is valued for its many healing properties. The colors in this collection are clear amber and yellow for brightness and warmth and yellow ocher for creativity.

The Soaps

- Citrus Honey Soap wrapped in plastic with paper labels decorated with bees
- Honey Soap in clear plastic wrap
- Flower Power Soaps with a silk leaf labels and resin bees to accent

Fragrant Companions

- Foaming Bath Salts in a muslin bag with a wooden scoop
- Botanical Bath Oil in a glass bottle with a bee on the cork
- Queen Bee Dusting Powder in a painted and decorated papier mache box

Finishing Touches

Other additions could include a rolled beeswax candle and a jar of honey. ❧

Provence Collection

Soap and water have been around for centuries, but it was the French who made soap special by triple milling it to create highly fragrant bars that smell sweet to the very end. The fragrant bouquets of scents in this collection — like Provence's fields of flowers — are calming and relaxing. The moss and olive greens and soft lavender are restful, tranquil, enchanting, and romantic colors.

The Soaps

- Rose & Olive Oil Soap wrapped in plastic wrap and tied with a ribbon around the sides
- Plaid Soap wrapped in a paper label and tied with jute
- Savon de Comte Soap wrapped like an extravagant gift with glassine paper and an old-fashioned soapmaker's sticker

Fragrant Companions

- Lavender Bath Salts in a pressed glass jar with a wooden scoop decorated with fleur de lis
- Lavender Bath Oil in long-necked decorative glass bottles
- Lavender Linen Sachets in a cloth envelope

Finishing Touches

- Candles, bundled and tied with beautiful fabric
- Cosmetic brushes and a lovely antique comb ❧

Renaissance Collection

Sensual and extravagant, this collection evokes exotic spices and riches from the new world. The mahogany browns and parchment colors are earthy, spicy, and rich.

The Soaps

- Rock Crystal Soaps packaged in a sheer gold drawstring bag
- Cardamom & Cinnamon Soap wrapped in plastic wrap with a paper label
- Tuscany Soap with a paper wrapper

Fragrant Companions

- Vanilla Bean Bath Salts in a glass jar
- Spicy Pear Potpourri with pear pomanders in a china dish with a lacy handkerchief
- Rose Bubble Bath in a cobalt blue bottle

Finishing Touches

- A soap dish made from a ceramic tile decoupaged with a classical painting (covered with a pour-on resin coating to make it practical)
- A square candle extravagantly decorated with a floral motif and gold leaf. ❧

Zen Harmony

A gift of tranquillity with an Asian theme. The restful greens are balanced with a little hint of stimulating red and rich gold.

The Soaps

- Green Tea Soap wrapped in plastic wrap with a handmade paper label and tied with red raffia
- Pebble Soaps on a bamboo soap dish
- Good Fortune Soap wrapped in plastic wrap with a paper label around the sides. Red raffia ties it together.
- Zen Bar with a handmade paper label, tied with red raffia and a Chinese coin

Fragrant Companions

- Spiced Chai Bath Bombs in a clear plastic bag
- Green Tub Tea packaged in handmade paper envelopes decorated with a Chinese character rubber stamp

Finishing Touches

Other additions could include a red votive candle in a glass container decorated with handmade paper and a gold Chinese character that says "Tao, the way." ❦

臺當儕頭真露芝化人
味一杷金尌柠攣桁

道

spiced chai

METRIC CONVERSION CHART

Inches to Millimeters and Centimeters

Inches	MM	CM
1/8	3	.3
1/4	6	.6
3/8	10	1.0
1/2	13	1.3
5/8	16	1.6
3/4	19	1.9
7/8	22	2.2
1	25	2.5
1-1/4	32	3.2
1-1/2	38	3.8
1-3/4	44	4.4
2	51	5.1
3	76	7.6
4	102	10.2
5	127	12.7
6	152	15.2
7	178	17.8
8	203	20.3
9	229	22.9
10	254	25.4
11	279	27.9
12	305	30.5

Yards to Meters

Yards	Meters
1/8	.11
1/4	.23
3/8	.34
1/2	.46
5/8	.57
3/4	.69
7/8	.80
1	.91
2	1.83
3	2.74
4	3.66
5	4.57
6	5.49
7	6.40
8	7.32
9	8.23
10	9.14

INDEX